TAMING THE GODS

TAMING THE GODS

*RELIGION AND DEMOCRACY
ON THREE CONTINENTS*

IAN BURUMA

PRINCETON UNIVERSITY PRESS
Princeton & Oxford

Published by Princeton University Press
41 William Street, Princeton, New Jersey 08540
In the United Kingdom: Princeton University Press, 6 Oxford Street, Woodstock, Oxfordshire OX20 1TW

Library of Congress Cataloging-in-Publication Data

Buruma, Ian.
Taming the gods : religion and democracy
on three continents / Ian Buruma.
p.   cm.
Includes bibliographical references (p.   ).
ISBN 978-0-691-13489-5 (hardcover : alk. paper)
1. Religion and state. 2. Democracy—Religious aspects.
3. United States—Religion. 4. Europe—Religion.
5. Japan—Religion. 6. China—Religion. I. Title.
BL65.S8B87 2010   322'.109—dc22
2009031550

British Library Cataloging-in-Publication Data is available

This book has been composed in ITC Caslon 224 Std

Printed on acid-free paper. ∞

press.princeton.edu

Printed in the United States of America

10 9 8 7 6 5 4 3 2 1

FOR MY FATHER,
S.L. BURUMA

CONTENTS

TAMING THE GODS

INTRODUCTION

The fact that religion is back is more newsworthy in Europe than in the United States, where religion was never supposed to have been away. But even in the United States, for about half a century between the 1920s and the 1970s, organized religion had not been a major political force. It was always there, especially outside the urban areas, as a social phenomenon. And it impinged on politics. John F. Kennedy, not an especially pious man, had to reassure the voters that he would never take orders from the Vatican. It would have been impossible for a candidate who openly professed disbelief to become president of the United States, and it still is. But Jimmy Carter's compulsion to spread the good news of his born-again faith was something of an anomaly. He was a political liberal, however, who never allowed religious authority to interfere with his politics. Since then, the influence of evangelical Christianity in the political arena has grown, mainly but not exclusively as a right-wing, socially conservative force.

Especially during the eight years of George W. Bush's administration, it was a commonplace in Europe to contrast the secular nature of the Old World to the religiosity of the United States. When the ideological positions that had hitched Western Europe and the United States together during the cold war became redundant after 1989, people began to sense a growing rift between the two continents, as though a schism had occurred in Western civilization. Forgetting just how recently the authority of established churches had been diminished even in the most liberal European countries, Europeans talked as though secularism had always distinguished them from the parochial, conservative, God-fearing Americans. It was an understandable perception, because even as the church lost most of its clout in Europe, the faithful gained more political power in the United States, at least in the Republican Party.

It is by no means a sure thing, however, that Christianity will not stage a comeback in Europe or retain its influence on politics in the United States. Even if the old established Catholic and Protestant churches in Europe do not manage to climb back to their former pinnacles of authority in social, cultural, and political affairs, it would be hard to say with certainty that evangelical movements will not appeal to Europeans, as they so evidently do to citizens on every other continent, including Asia. Perhaps it is true that prosperity makes people less eager to be reborn in the bosom of Christ, but who is to say that Europeans will always be as rich as they are now? And the increasing wealth of the south of the United States does not seem to have diminished the appetite for religion among some of its richer denizens, including at least two former presidents.

Radical secularists often assume that any organized faith poses a threat to liberal democracy. In cases where religious authority assumes political authority, this threat is real. Democratic politics are a matter of resolving conflicting interests through negotiation and compromise. A religious institution claiming to represent absolute or divine truth cannot make these necessary compromises without the danger of corrupting its own principles, never mind political ones. This is why devout Christians, mainly

Protestants, in Europe as well as the United States were often the first to advocate the separation between church and state—to protect the integrity of their faith.

Although it would be absurd to claim that organized religion is incompatible with liberal democracy, tensions between religious and secular authority remain. My book is an attempt to sort out, in different cultures, how democracies have been affected, for better or worse, by these tensions. I do not assume to cover all religions, in all countries. That would be an impossible task. I have concentrated on Western Europe and the United States, as well as the two countries in Asia that I know best, Japan and China. One of my main guides in this venture is a great European thinker who wrote a classic about the United States of America, and even had interesting things to say about Islam: Alexis de Tocqueville. In his view, democracy in the United States could be established *because* Americans shared a Christian faith, specifically a Protestant faith, whose free agents observed clear boundaries between their churches and the democratic state. Tocqueville was worried, for good reason, that matters in Europe were not quite so simple. There, particularly in Catholic nations, religious claims were often seen as a barrier to democratic rule.

My book consists of three parts, one on church and state relations in Europe and the United States, one on religious authority in China and Japan, and one on the challenges of Islam in contemporary Europe. The thread that runs through these inquiries, despite their wide diversity in space and time, is the question posed by Tocqueville: what is needed, apart from freedom of speech and the right to vote, to hold democratic societies together? Is the rule of law enough, or do we need common values, ethics, mores? And what is the role of religion in all this; is it a help or a hindrance to liberal democracy?

What Tocqueville could never have foreseen was the rise of Islam as a major factor in European politics. Even though, statistically, pious Muslims only constitute a small minority of European citizens, Islam is a close rival to Christianity in some areas as the largest organized religion. Exactly what this means in terms of social or political authority is hard to measure, since unlike Roman Catholicism or established Protestant denominations, there is no Muslim Church, with a comparable hierarchy of priests. It would be difficult for most Muslims to establish a common program; their cultures, backgrounds, interests, and beliefs are too diverse, which is one reason why there are, as yet, no Muslim political parties in Europe. But still, practicing Muslims, including the majority of law-abiding believers who have no truck with any violent political ideology, are posing a challenge to the secular certainties gained by Europeans in the last thirty years or so.

Europeans—and perhaps to a lesser extent Americans—are afraid of the consequences. Populist warnings of being "out-bred" or "swamped" by Muslims are finding a receptive audience. Some writers, caught up in (and helping stir up) this mood of anxiety, speak of "Eurabia," as though Europe, too weak or unwilling to defend its own civilization, were in danger of becoming "Islamized" by people who not only are more than willing to fight for their beliefs, but are producing many more children, at a much faster rate, than "we" are. The assumption here is that even if this were true, which is by no means sure, the grandchildren of the current breeders will be a carbon copy, in terms of culture and religion, of the current generation. An unlikely prospect.

It is not always easy to distinguish fear of an alien faith, a faith moreover with which Christendom has been at war in the past, from fear of aliens *tout court*. To some Europeans it doesn't matter whether a Muslim believes in the Prophet, let alone whether he is a holy warrior, for he or she is a dark-skinned foreigner, and that is quite threatening enough. Some people fear that our very civilization is at stake when "their" customs, which may or may not have a religious background, clash with our present notions of how decent citizens should behave. This is why former liberals, who once prided themselves on their vigilance against racism, sometimes see eye to eye with cultural conservatives in their opposition to Islam. For Islam, as they see it, with its antiquated ideas on homosexuality, or the role of women, threatens to overthrow the very gains that progressives fought for in the last century. Hence the hysteria over women wearing body-covering burkas, even in countries where the number of such women is minimal.

No doubt some Muslims do hold views that fall short of contemporary secular norms. The same goes for some Jews, and some Christians, not to mention pockets of cultures frozen in time, such as the Amish or the American Mennonites. The reason people find Muslims especially frightening is their relative number in concentrated areas of European cities and the fusion, sometimes real, sometimes imagined, between these customary views and violent political ideologies. The brutality of radical political Islam has already left its bloody tracks in several European countries. But it is all too common to simply assume that the bearded man in ankle-length trousers or the woman in a black *hijab* is hiding an assassin's knife or a ticking bomb.

Relations between church and state, or religious and secular authority, cannot be explained as abstractions. They can only be understood in the context of history. Since it is my intention to try and make sense of the world we live in, rather than to write a polemic, history, and thinkers in history, will form a large part of my account.

Because European countries have different histories, in terms of church-state relations and social behavior, societies grapple with the large presence of Muslims in different ways. Britain favors a social form of laissez-faire. People are entitled to stick to their own ways, as long as they abide by the law. British liberals, perhaps haunted by colonial guilt, have sometimes gone further and positively encouraged people to conserve their traditions, since any pressure to conform to British customs would smack of imperialist arrogance. Guilt, in this case, hides a peculiar irony, for this type of "multiculturalism," much hated by conservatives, actually reflects the way much of the British Empire was governed, by dividing colonial subjects into communal groups, and ruling through their leaders. This, in turn, is in line with British traditions: religion, even the established Anglican Church, is seen in cultural more than theological terms. To be an Anglican does not demand belief so much as conformity to certain national customs. Why deny similar cultural allegiances to someone of Pakistani or Bangladeshi origin?

The Dutch, too, used to think of faith in terms of multiculturalism, long before that word was known. Each to his or her own, Protestant, Catholic, or Jew. In the Netherlands this idea used to be the applied to all aspects of life: a Catholic went to Catholic schools, Catholic football clubs, Catholic universities, Catholic social clubs. Catholics married Catholics, voted for Catholic political parties, listened to Catholic radio stations, and retired on the proceeds of Catholic pension funds. The same was true of the many Protestant denominations. And liberals and socialists had their own separate worlds as well. At the top of the social and political system, paternalistic representatives of the various "pillars" would work out a consensus on national policies, usually behind closed doors. This "pillar system" was more or less invented in the nineteenth century to stop believers from going for one another's throats. It made democracy work.

Since the French Revolution was in part a rebellion against the authority of the Catholic Church, the French republic is ideologically committed to secularism in a way the British and the Dutch are not. Public places, such as state schools, cannot allow religious symbols to challenge their secular nature. And the republican idea of the *citoyen*, equal before the law, an individual component of the general will, does not allow for a view that makes communal distinctions. Multiculturalism is anathema to the ideology of the French republic. Many people fear that the smallest concession to religious expression in the public or political sphere might revive the power of the hated priests.

Even if relations with Muslims are less fraught in the United States, the questions of church and state are hardly resolved. The rift between those who believe that the United States always was and always should remain a Christian (or Judeo-Christian) nation, and those who agree with Thomas Jefferson that the state is neutral and religion a wholly private affair, still runs deep. This is complicated by the fact that conservative American Christians, like their European counterparts, sometimes feel more akin to conservative Muslims than to secular liberals, whose wickedness, in the eyes of the believers, is the main threat to decent society.

It is often assumed that the vexing problem of religious dogmatism in politics is strictly due to monotheistic traditions. Only believers in one God become violently intolerant of other beliefs. And theocracy is something more commonly associated with Christian or Muslim faiths, based as they are on bookish dogmas, than with Hinduism, Taoism, or Buddhism.

The truth, as usual, is more complicated. Although believers in one God (except for the Jews) have a greater desire to spread their faith universally—since their God is a universal and not a tribal or local one—the problem of church and state, how to separate political from religious authority, can be just as acute in polytheistic countries. The Tibetan tradition, and the position of the Dalai Lama in contemporary politics, is an example that comes to mind. But it is not the only one. I will examine the examples of China and Japan in some detail to show how the politics of belief have been dealt with there, and how religious faith may have helped or hindered the development of Asian democratic institutions.

This is not unrelated to problems in the West. First of all, as relative power shifts to the East, politics in Asia will have an increasing impact on life elsewhere. But more important in terms of intellectual history, China in particular has often been held up as a mirror (highly distorted, to be sure) to the West by Western thinkers disenchanted by conditions at home. Voltaire, among others, assumed that China's political system, based on secular Confucian ethics, was more rational, that is, less encumbered by religious authority, and thus superior to the way France was ruled. Similar assumptions were made in the Maoist years, even as China was in the murderous grip of a quasi-religious insanity.

The paradox here is that both China and Japan have been idealized in the West, not only for the supposed rationalism of Confucian politics but also for the superior spirituality of their religious traditions: Zen, Taoism, and the like.

Parts of the Confucian world—Japan, South Korea, and Taiwan—are now ruled by democratically elected governments. Vietnam and China are not. My attempt to take a closer look at the role played by religious institutions in these developments is not just meant as a way to delve into East Asian history, fascinating though it is, but also as a way to gain further insights into the tangled relations between religious faith and secular politics. Are certain faiths more conducive to democratic politics than others? Does monotheism indeed contain greater ideological dangers than more flexible beliefs?

Not having had either the benefits—or miseries—of a religious upbringing (we belonged to the "liberal pillar"), I cannot write as a partisan of any faith. Nor do I have a special preference for polytheism over monotheism, even though I can see the wisdom of hedging one's bets by backing more than one god. I am not a militant atheist but duck behind the safe screen of agnosticism when challenged. I am persuaded of one thing, however: I do not think religious faith, the desire for metaphysical answers to questions that cannot be rationally answered, the need for and delight in mystical ritual and spiritual speculation, will go away. Nor am I persuaded that they should.

Attempts to crush organized faith with force have rarely resulted in peace, let alone democracy. On the contrary, they caused violent religious rebellions or produced political cults no less murderous than the worst religious violence. Since the subject of this essay is religion and democracy, I have left such quasi-religious political movements as Nazism and Stalinism aside. But they show clearly what happens when the state claims to be the source of absolute truth. Such claims, when backed with force, are always lethal, whether they are enforced by commissars or by priests.

Religion is not a rational enterprise. Its metaphysical claims cannot be proven; either one believes them or one does not. When reflecting on the problems of religion and democracy, the main issue is how to stop irrational passions from turning violent. Spinoza, not a religious man, believed that religion was fine, but only under certain strict conditions. Faith should make people behave lovingly and peacefully, should never get mixed up in rational inquiry, and should always be controlled by rulers of the secular state. I'm not sure I agree with the last point, but the first two are unimpeachable.

ONE

FULL TENTS AND EMPTY CATHEDRALS

"Elmer Gantry was drunk. He was eloquently drunk, lovingly and pugnaciously drunk." So goes the beginning of Sinclair Lewis's novel about the evangelical preacher Elmer Gantry, a great American character, boundless in his greed, a sinner obsessed with the Devil, a salesman of astonishing energy who believes in the greater good of his own success, a man of great charm and destructive power. It is difficult to imagine Gantry as a European. He is too capacious, too full of enthusiasm, too careless about fate, class, and tradition. In short, Elmer "Hellcat" Gantry is way too optimistic to be anything but a full-blooded American.

Lewis wrote his book in 1926 as an indictment of American evangelical fervor. He dedicated it to H. L. Mencken, the journalistic scourge of rural boobies, boosters, and religious hucksters. We are not supposed to admire Gantry. Indeed, we should fear him and the people who believe in hustlers like him. And yet, especially in the movie version, with the magnificent Burt Lancaster, it is difficult not to admire Gantry a little, or even to like him. Playing on people's fear of death (the main source of his power), the preacher, like the culture that spawned him, is brimming with vitality.

The novel, as well as the film, begins, as all good stories about American preachers do, with the hero as a sinner, a drunk who sweet-talks women into shabby hotel beds only to abandon them the next morning. Folks who have found Christ like their preachers to have been sinners: that way they can identify with them; they feel like sinners themselves and live in hope of redemption. But unlike many crowd-pulling preachers, Gantry did not start as an amateur. He acquired the taste for preaching ever since he was prompted by his devout mother during Annual Prayer Week to get on his knees at the Baptist church and confess his sins: "He was certain that he would never again want

13

to guzzle, to follow loose women, to blaspheme; he knew the rapture of salvation—yes, and of being the center of interest in the crowd."[1]

Gantry is later ordained in Paris, Kansas, as minister of the gospel in the Baptist Church while studying at the Mizpah Theological Seminary until he gets kicked out for spending Easter Sunday at a drunken orgy with a bunch of businessmen at the Ishawonga Hotel in the town of Monarch.

The successful evangelical preacher combines a talent for showmanship, business acumen, and a plausible air of sincerity. Scholarship is a drawback in this line of work. Learning, if acquired at all, should be disguised. The point is to be a man of the people, a regular guy, and not some stuck-up, college-educated snob who thinks he is better than the rest of us. The latter type, in Lewis's novel, is represented by the Reverend Cecil Aylston, a High Church man, English (of course), educated at Oxford. He is in fact no better than Gantry: an adulterer, a forger, and a drunk, forced to seek his fortune in the New World. But he puts on gentlemanly airs and is the devoted assistant and teacher of Sharon Falconer, a pretty young preacher whom he has instructed in the use of proper English grammar and encouraged to tone down the histrionics. Gantry took one look at Sister Sharon and instantly became Aylston's rival for her affections.

By then, after a stint as a salesman of agricultural tools, Gantry had taken up professional preaching again. He is promoted as "a power in the machinery world." His sermon to the good people of Lincoln, advertised as "Increasing Sales with God and the Gideons," promises to be "a revelation of the new world of better business."

There is no need to vulgarize the flock, says Aylston, in his mincing English accent. But Gantry understands that this is precisely what is needed, even though he wouldn't put it quite that way: "The good old-fashioned hell," that's what people want. Sister Sharon takes his advice and, as usual with Gantry, ends up in his bed. Coached by her lover, she becomes wildly successful as a charismatic faith healer, telling people to drop their crutches and walk with the Lord (until they drop to the floor, out of sight of the ecstatic believers). Together Brother Elmer and Sister Sharon rake in the cash. But it doesn't last. Her world literally goes up in smoke, when a smoldering cigarette lights up her prayer tent. She dies after trying to assure the panic-stricken mob that the Lord will help her lead them safely through the flames.

The death of Sister Sharon marks the end of the movie, but not the novel. Gantry is irrepressible. Nothing will deter him in his ambition to draw bigger crowds, to make more money. No story about an American evangelical preacher is complete without a serious scandal—usually followed by redemption. Satan must have the penultimate word. So it is with Gantry, who is married by now. A sordid affair with his secretary, who attempts to blackmail him with the help of a small-time hood, is exposed in the papers. Gantry does what all good sinners do. He goes to his church and falls on his knees, stretching his arms to his flock, sobbing. And with him "they all knelt and sobbed and prayed, while outside the locked glass of the church, seeing the mob kneel within, hundreds knelt on the steps of the church, on the sidewalk, all down the block."

> "Oh, my friends!" cried Elmer, "do you believe in my innocence, in the fiendishness of my accusers? Reassure me with a hallelujah!"
> The church thundered with the triumphant hallelujah, and in a sacred silence Elmer prayed.

And he prays, and prays, against Satan, and for the freedom from all temptations. Then, just as he turns to include the choir in his entreaties to the Lord, he spots "a new singer, a girl with charming ankles and lively eyes," and vows to make her acquaintance. But he doesn't let this thought interrupt the paean of his prayer for more than an instant.

> Let me count this day, Lord, as the beginning of a new and more vigorous life, as the beginning of a crusade for complete morality and the domination of the Christian church through all the land. Dear Lord, thy work is but begun! We shall yet make these United States a moral nation![2]

Sinclair Lewis is not a subtle novelist. His message leaves no room for ambiguities. Yet Elmer Gantry is an unforgettable character who seems like a crude caricature until one has seen his real-life colleagues on television. Examples of contemporary Gantrys are not confined to the evangelical stages. They appear in all their pomp at political party conventions in election years. Ronald Reagan had some of Gantry in him, even though he was not very religious; so had Bill Clinton and, despite his lack of natural charisma, George W. Bush, a man who exemplified to many Americans the hard road from sin to redemption. The difference between selling the gospel, agricultural machinery, or a political candidate is not always obvious in the United States. For all mix show business with popular sentiment, the reassuring air of the regular guy, and the braggadocio of the carnival huckster.

When Rush Limbaugh, a Gantry figure if there ever was one, was interviewed at his palatial Florida mansion about his extraordinary success as a right-wing political radio jockey, he explained what drove him: "Not my political ideas. Conservatism didn't buy this house. First and foremost I'm a businessman. My first goal is to attract the largest possible audience so I can charge confiscatory ad rates. I happen to have great entertainment skills, but that enables me to sell airtime."[3] These words might have been written by Sinclair Lewis, and quite possibly we might have faulted him for laying it on too thick.

In fact, Lewis's book caused such a scandal when it was published that it put evangelical preachers on the defensive. Elmer Gantry embarrassed them—that and the Scopes Monkey trial in 1925, when a high school teacher in Tennessee was prosecuted for teaching Darwin's theory of evolution, which made Pentacostalists and other holy-rolling fundamentalists look foolish. Partly as a result, they shied away from politics. And yet they still managed to cast such a long shadow over American life that when the movie version of *Elmer Gantry* came out in 1960, the producers added a message that young and impressionable children should be shielded from the contents of the film.

•   •   •

When Europeans watch American television, they are often astonished by the money-grubbing crassness of the present-day Elmer Gantrys. Here, they think, is a culture that truly divides the New World from the Old: the sheer vulgarity of the howling, sweating televangelists and the primitive notion of America as a land blessed by God, a City on the Hill, inhabited by a chosen people, glassy-eyed, in double-knit suits.

Not just religion but American democracy itself appears to be corrupted by this type of commercial boosterism. People call the United States a democracy, but Americans don't vote for their own good or along the lines of political reason but for candidates who are most successfully marketed, like movie stars or products backed by huge commercial enterprises. Venal ambition comes wrapped up in showbiz. When you add to this mix the puritanical goals of businessmen-preachers whose sermons are eagerly lapped up by millions of television viewers, Gantry's victory seems to be complete; the borders between church and state have been fatally breached. Or so it seems to many Europeans, as well as American liberals. There are plenty of examples to back this view. But is it the whole picture?

It is easy to forget that revivalism actually began in Europe, as did the idea of God-chosen countries. To Dutch Protestants rebelling against Catholic Spain in the sixteenth century, their republic was the new Zion. Scottish Presbyterians and Irish Protestants believed that they had a covenant with God in their struggle against papism. German Pietists in the seventeenth century and English Methodists, Shakers, and other dissenters in the eighteenth century preached that every man had his own pipeline to the Lord and salvation did not come from membership in established churches or need the mediation of official clerics.

The First Great Awakening in eighteenth-century America was led by an English evangelist named George Whitefield, who drew huge crowds wherever he appeared from New England to Georgia. Whitefield was a born actor. David Garrick, who attended one of his prayer meetings in England, was particularly impressed by his vivid portrayals of biblical characters. Whitefield sang and danced and hollered, leaving the crowds begging for more. His American colleague, Jonathan Edwards, is perhaps better known today. Edwards's passionate sermons about God's wrath against sinners were famous for making people swoon and faint. But of the two, people who saw them recalled, the Englishman was the more inclined to pull out all the stops.

However, even though the roots of American evangelical faith are in Europe, and Europeans were the first to spread the good word, it really came into its own in the New World. In the mid-nineteenth century, the established Anglican and Congregationalist churches of the early colonists had already been overtaken by Baptists, Methodists, Presbyterians, and other sectarians roaming the land of cabins and prayer meetings. They were followed by Pentacostalists, Restorationists, and charismatic healers, dancing and jerking, and speaking in tongues, while attendance at the old churches was shrinking. The trend has continued to this day. A Gallup Poll in 2004 found that 43 to 46 percent of Americans think of themselves as born-again Christians, and 77 percent of American Christians believe in Hell and 70 percent in Satan. Meanwhile in France, a largely Catholic country, less than 20 percent even bother to attend Mass. In the rest of Europe many of the most ancient churches and cathedrals are kept open for tourists, while the less distinguished ones are turned into chic apartment buildings or mosques. This is why more and more liberal Europeans sneer at America, especially when a president presents himself as a born-again sin and redemption man.

Scorn for the culture of the United States has a long history in Europe, to be sure. When a famous Dutch writer named Menno ter Braak published an essay in 1928 titled *Why I Disdain "America,"* without ever having set foot there, no one found this remarkable. *Amerikanismus* (Heidegger's term) was seen by Ter Braak and other conservatives as a threat to European civilization. It was shallow, devoid of high culture, greedy, obsessed with meretricious fame, and so on. An excess of religiosity was usually not something cultural conservatives in Europe held against the materialistic New World. Today's European critics of the United States, however, who cite evangelical

19

fervor as one of the reasons for their disdain, sound much like Menno Ter Braak. Evangelical zeal has to be the result of deep ignorance, cultural emptiness, and an addiction to celebrity and primitive pizzazz.

There is, however, another possible explanation for the success of popular faith that throws a less negative light on the American scene. The peculiar forms that Christian faith has taken in the United States are in fact closely linked to American democracy. Alexis de Tocqueville, an aristocrat who celebrated the birth of democracy while fearing some of its consequences, wrote that the religious atmosphere was the first thing that struck him on arrival in the United States. A pious Catholic himself, he approved of religion; indeed, he thought it was indispensible to maintain social stability, especially in a democracy. For moral ties had to be tightened, in his view, when political ties were relaxed. And this could only be done through religious faith.

Tocqueville traveled in America during the Second Great Awakening, when Mormons, Seventh-day Adventists, and Jehovah's Witnesses headed for the western frontier. It was a time of camp meetings: lonely settlers from isolated outposts would gather for weeks at a time, dancing and praying for salvation. Two things struck Tocqueville about the religious atmosphere he encountered. One was the devotion to liberty: "For the Americans the ideas of Christianity and liberty are so completely mingled that it is almost impossible to get them to conceive of the one without the other; it is not a question with them of sterile beliefs bequeathed by the past and vegetating rather than living in the depths of the soul."[4] This was in contrast to Europe. In France, wrote Tocqueville, "I had seen the spirits of religion and of freedom almost always marching in opposite directions. In America I found them intimately linked together in joint reign over the same land."[5]

The other thing he noted was the worldly character of much religious preaching. While paying proper attention to the future life, American preachers freely allowed their followers "to give some of their hearts' care to the needs of the present, apparently considering the good things of this world as objects of some, albeit secondary importance."[6] The "honest pursuit of prosperity" was clearly seen as a good thing. The pursuit of material success and hope for salvation in the next world were not distinct, but closely linked. It is a point Tocqueville might have made about Protestantism in Europe, too, but in the United States he found that this was the dominant ethos even of the Catholic faith.

The reason why Americans were so religious, while in Europe the churches were under attack (to Tocqueville's evident dismay), was the severance in the United States of church and state. "I have no hesitation," wrote Tocqueville, "in stating that throughout my stay in America I met nobody, lay or cleric, who did not agree about that."[7] He thought it was especially important in democracies not only to have strong faith but also to keep it well away from worldly power, because political theories, not to mention political leaders, come and go. If the Americans, "who have handed over the world of politics to the experiments of innovators, had not placed religion beyond their reach, what could it hold on to in the ebb and flow of human opinions?"[8]

In other words, Americans felt that they could believe freely, not just because religious freedom was protected by the Constitution but because religious authority was not in the hands of worldly politicians. Again, Tocqueville points out the difference with Europe in one of the most important passages of *Democracy in America*: "Unbelievers in Europe attack Christians more as political than as religious enemies; they hate faith as the opinion of a party much more than as a mistaken belief, and they reject the clergy less because they are the representatives of God than because they are the friends of authority."[9]

The third thing noticed by Tocqueville about American religious practices was the lack of traditional flimflam, of smells and bells, of robes, miters, and other signs of rank, or deference to custom. The Great Awakenings, all the barking and swooning and fainting notwithstanding, were an assault on the authority of established churches as much as French Jacobinism was, even though it was considerably less violent. The aim of French revolutionaries was to build a secular republic on the ashes of the oppressive Catholic Church. Most of them were opposed to the church that baptized them. But they did not seek alternative ways to Jerusalem, in freelance churches. For the face of God still bore the features of the hated priests.

Americans, too, revolted against the established church. In New England, for example, where Anglicanism was the official religion and heresy was still a capital offense in the eighteenth century, people were burned at the stake for their godlessness. Thomas Jefferson, himself raised in the English Church, made it clear that worldly powers should have no authority over matters of faith: "our rulers can have authority over such natural rights only as we have submitted to them. The rights of conscience we never submitted, we could not submit. We are answerable for them to our God. The legitimate powers of government extend to such acts only as are injurious to others. But it does me no injury for my neighbour to say there are twenty gods, or no god. It neither picks my pocket nor breaks my leg."[10]

Jefferson was a man of the Enlightenment, a Francophile who believed passionately in reason. He was probably less religious than Tocqueville, but in regards to religious

freedom his cause was the same as that of the Restorationists, the "New Lights" Congregationalists, and other Protestants of the Great Awakening, who believed that men
could be born again through God's grace and held no truck
with the hierarchy of Old World churches. Jefferson may
have had nothing much in common with the charismatic
holy-rollers and fire-and-brimstone preachers of Georgia
or upstate New York, but when it came to their freedom to
believe whatever they wanted, in any way they wanted, he
was entirely on their side.

Elmer Gantry's scorn for the pretensions of Cecil
Aylston was shared by the early revivalists who set up
shop along the new frontier. As Frank Lambert, historian
of the Great Awakening, put it: "The spirit of the American
Revolution tilted toward New Light individualism, encouraging an 'egalitarian theology' and a 'Christianity of the
people.'... [They] insisted that, as in politics, in religion
all are on equal footing before God."[11]

This was true of course only up to a point—the main
point being slavery. George Whitefield was unusual for his
time in that he preached to slaves and prayed for their
salvation. But he was not opposed to the system and even
owned a few slaves himself while living in Georgia. However, Tocqueville had another insight that still helps us understand something about America today. Shocked by the
violence of the French Revolution, Tocqueville was fasci-
nated by why other societies avoided such a cataclysmic
event, especially aristocratic England with its vast differences in standing and wealth. Religion had to have something to do with it. Catholicism, he mused, "may dispose
the faithful to obedience, but it does not prepare them
for inequality. However, I would say that Protestantism in
general orients men much less toward equality than toward independence."[12]

So not only did the evangelical brand of American Protestantism favor histrionic emotion over superior learning and democracy over authoritarianism, but it was also a brand of individualism that tolerated inequality as long as men were free to compete for "the good things of this world." Some forms of American evangelism were (and still are) actively opposed to capitalism, but one can see why free religious enterprise could also be used to promote it. Perhaps it was precisely because people were convinced that they, or at least all white folks, were equal before God that they could live more easily with being unequal in this world. A Marxist would say, with some justice, that this is precisely why capitalists have a reason to promote that faith.

A system that promotes economic and political freedom does not, however, exclude moral bigotry. The puritan ethics that Tocqueville saw as the bedrock of American society and a necessary condition for building stable democratic institutions in the United States also bred a degree of social conformity that dismayed him. Like all survivors of revolutionary violence, Tocqueville was fearful of mass conformity, which could easily lead to mob rule. The same people, who insisted on their individual rights as citizens of a democratic republic, were capable of inflicting horrific violence on others on the basis of their sexual practices or simply the color of their skin. Religion has often been used to justify such savagery.

Europeans, though less prone, in recent times, to turn to God as an ally, have stained their history with even more blood than the Americans. And the establishment of democracies in Europe has been, on the whole, a more painful process. Religion has had much to do with this. The question is, however, whether this reveals a rift between the Old World and the New World or more between religious traditions that cut across that wide watery divide.

24

• • •

As the First Great Awakening was taking place in the United States in the middle of the eighteenth century, David Hume wrote his essay "Of Superstition and Enthusiasm." It is in some ways a surprising essay for a man of his conservative temperament, though not untypical of certain English prejudices. Hume, like Spinoza a century earlier, had little respect for any form of religion. All religion is "false," as far as he was concerned, but he made some interesting distinctions and was more inclined than Spinoza to recognize the importance of religious institutions. There were two kinds of believers, in his view: the superstitious and the enthusiasts. The former tend to be fearful, melancholy, even abject, and thus much too timorous to approach the Divinity by themselves. This is why, in Hume's words, "superstition is favorable to priestly power."[13]

Enthusiasts, on the other hand, are drawn to irrationality by a surfeit of self-confidence: "Hope, pride, presumption, a warm imagination, together with ignorance, are, therefore, the true sources of enthusiasm." While the superstitious turn anxiously to churchly authority for mediation between Man and God, enthusiasts "have been free from the yoke of ecclesiastics, and have expressed great independence of devotion; with a contempt of forms, ceremonies, and traditions." More than that: "The fanatic consecrates himself and bestows on his own person a sacred character, much superior to what forms and ceremonious institutions can confer on any other."

Not a bad description of the European—and especially the American—evangelicals. As typical examples of religious fanaticism Hume mentions the early Quakers in England, followed by the Presbyterians, the Anabaptists in Germany, and the Camisards in France. But fanaticism,

Hume observes, is hard to sustain for very long. And so he concludes: "Religions, which partake of enthusiasm are, on their first rise, more furious and violent than those which partake of superstition; but in a little time become more gentle and moderate."

Of the different falsehoods, superstition is the more dangerous, as it "steals in gradually and insensibly; renders men tame and submissive; is acceptable to the magistrate, and seems inoffensive to the people: Till at last the priest, having firmly established his authority, becomes the tyrant and disturber of human society, by his endless contentions, persecutions, and religious wars." Hence his observation that "superstition is an enemy to civil liberty, and enthusiasm a friend to it," because the latter destroys ecclesiastical power, even as the superstitious "groan under the dominion of priests."

Having enjoyed the blessings of a patriotic Dutch education, which included a great deal of Protestant propaganda against the evils of Catholic Spain, I cannot but see merit in Hume's analysis. And yet the furious and violent stages of religious enthusiasm can disturb human society just as much as priestly despotism and, far from dissipating, have a way of coming back. One does not have to be a ferocious anti-American to see evangelical enthusiasm behind the hubristic attempts to transform the world by force. And besides, the violence unleashed in the religious wars of seventeenth-century Europe was hardly the sole responsibility of tyrannical priests. Nor can Protestant savagery be ascribed simply to an early burst of enthusiasm. And as far as tyranny is concerned, Spinoza was surely right to see Cromwell as an equally authoritarian ruler as the king he violently replaced. Hume, to be fair, saw Cromwell as a dangerous enthusiast as well, but one who also brought more liberty.

Like Hobbes and Spinoza before him, Hume was concerned about taming the violent passions of religious believers, as well as stopping religious irrationality from interfering with rational inquiry, two essential conditions for any democratic system to succeed. Hume believed that once the violent stage was over, a more liberal Protestant version of Christianity could contribute to political liberty, but only if the wild, intolerant, and superstitious elements of religion were kept firmly in check. He was a great believer in institutions, including the established church. The Anglican Church was necessary, in his view, for the stability of English society, and this included the civil liberties the English people were fortunate enough to enjoy.

Hume's conservatism was a typical example of English compromise. An agnostic on miracles and deeply suspicious of all clerics, Hume did not accept that morality was God-given. He believed in the use of reason and was a promoter of science and philosophy, which he never confused with theology. But reason was not enough to explain everything. Nature and human life were too full of mysteries. And if morality could not be based entirely on human reason, nor could political institutions. In extreme cases, people were entitled to rebel against a tyrant, but "the people" could no more choose their system of government than their native languages or cultural habits. Political legitimacy was neither divinely ordained nor a matter of popular sovereignty but of tradition, history, sentiment, prejudice, and institutions grown over time. Precisely because he was a man of the Enlightenment, Hume was convinced that nothing could be known absolutely. That is why man needs custom and tradition to guide him. This is the basis of British "mixed government," of anchoring society in the established church, the aristocracy, the monarchy, and an elected parliament—not because God willed it so but because man needs it.

Hobbes and Spinoza were more radical. Since morality is not determined by a higher being, men in the state of nature, as conceived by Hobbes, are ruled by their desires, their fears, and their ignorance. This can only result in anarchy and perpetual warfare—"the life of man, solitary, poor, nasty, brutish, and short."[14] Religious strife occurs because men, in their dark ignorance, will follow priests, prophets, and seers, who promote competing metaphysical recipes to ease their fears. The only thing for it, then, is to establish an absolute worldly authority, which will crush these competing superstitions, take control of the church, and impose moral behavior by force. This way there would be peace, order, and room for rational thinkers to search for the truth unhindered by the peddlers of irrationality.

Hobbes was one of the authors in Christian Europe of "the Great Separation."[15] Following in the footsteps of Machiavelli, he introduced a science of politics based on secular interests, divorced from metaphysical justifications. The only way for man to be delivered from the brutal state of nature, and the dangerous blandishments of religious pied pipers, was to have a political system ruled by an enlightened tyrant—secular, and decidedly undemocratic.

Spinoza took a similar view of the state of nature but came to a different, far more democratic conclusion. In Spinoza's state of nature, it is every man for himself. There is no such thing as good or bad, whether or not divinely decreed. Survival is all that matters, and no one can feel safe in a state where all is permitted and everyone is a potential enemy. Cooperation, alliances, laws, and society are necessary conditions for "supporting life and cultivating the mind." Not only that, but even "natural right" is only conceivable when "men have general rights, and combine to defend the possession of the lands they inhabit and cultivate, to protect themselves, to repel all violence, and to live according to the general judgment of all." This is what Spinoza calls "dominion."[16]

However, unlike Hobbes, Spinoza did not favor a tyrannical form of dominion, an aristocratic one, or even a mixed one, like Hume, but a democracy, by which he meant something reasonably close to what we understand by that term today: "For all, who are born of citizen parents, or on the soil of the country, or who have deserved well of the republic, or have accomplished any other conditions upon which the law grants to a man right of citizenship; they all, I say, have a right to demand for themselves the right to vote in the supreme council and to fill public offices, nor can they be refused it, but for crime or infamy."[17]

Religious believers have often denounced Spinoza, or "Spinozism," as being anti-religious or atheist. He was indeed an atheist in the sense that he did not believe in a deity who created and guided the cosmos. God, in his mind, was another word for nature. But he was not anti-religion per se. Spinoza recognized that religious belief could promote love and charity. But the state had no right to tell us what to believe. In his words: "The care of propagating religion should be left to God, or the supreme authorities, upon whom alone falls the charge of affairs of state."[18] This sounds a little muddled. If the state has no business telling us what to believe, why should it have any more business promoting belief? The only answer can be that, above all, Spinoza wanted the state to control the church, even when it came to promoting the faith. But the state had no right to tell citizens *what* faith to adopt, or indeed to adopt any particular faith at all.

Religion, in other words, is a private affair, but its propagation cannot be left to the churches. Spinoza left no room for autonomous religious institutions—that would have opened the way to priestly abuse of power. He did not wish to grant churches any special privileges: no land, no tax breaks, no authority over religious doctrine, no right to censor opinions, and so on. This was a radical position, considering the time and place in which he held it (seventeenth-century Holland, where the churches were very powerful indeed). Too radical for most countries, even today.

The excellent scholar of Dutch history, Jonathan Israel, has made a strong case that the radical "Early Enlightenment" of Spinoza was the truly democratic one.[19] Later Enlightenment thinkers, such as Hume and Locke, watered down the intellectual achievements of the seventeenth-century radicals by making too many compromises, in terms of class privileges, as well as organized faith. Spinoza really did think that everyone should be free to believe—or not believe—whatever he wished, as long as he did not break the law or cause harm to others. Locke, on the other hand, barely tolerated Catholics, was suspicious of Jews, and did not tolerate atheists.

From Israel's keenly Spinozist perspective, the "mixed governments" of the British and Dutch monarchies, one with an established church protected by the sovereign and the other with a plethora of church-affiliated political parties, are the diminished heirs of the compromised late Enlightenment. They are better than tyrannies, to be sure, but not as good as they ought to have been, and certainly not as good as received Anglo-Saxon opinion thinks they are. The French republic had higher ideals, more in line with the Early Enlightenment, which was the source, Israel writes, "of the strand of republicanism which developed ultimately into Jacobinism, and attempted, after 1789, to eradicate monarchy, social hierarchy, and ecclesiastical power by means of revolution."[20]

The link is clearly there, even though Spinoza was not as dogmatic as the Jacobins about politics or religion. But there is no doubt that the French Revolution crushed organized religion and paved the way for political arrangements that were more secularist[21] than existed anywhere else at the time. The question is whether these arrangements were also more democratic, or liberal, than the mixed governments of other European states. And it is not clear either that opposing the Catholic Church meant a real reduction in faith. Perhaps it merely displaced it.

•   •   •

In 1989, the fateful year of democratic revolts against communist tyranny, François Mitterrand, as president of France, invited his fellow European leaders to celebrate the bicentenary of the French Revolution. It looked as though the whole world had come to Paris, streaming down the Champs Elysées, Europeans, Americans, Africans, but also Chinese refugees from the failed Tiananmen Rebellion, to pay tribute to France as the *patrie* of Fraternity, Equality, and Liberty. Forgetting, for a moment, Robespierre and the Terror, the French Revolution, and especially the Declaration of the Rights of Man and of the Citizen, as proclaimed in the National Assembly in April 1789, were officially presented as the quasi-sacred sources of democratic freedom in the world. Only Margaret Thatcher, one of the official guests, tried to put a damper on the joyful mood by pointing out that British freedoms owed nothing to France and everything to the Magna Carta.

Writing brilliantly about the occasion in the *New York Review of Books*, the Irish intellectual Conor Cruise O'Brien made a similar point more amusingly. First of all, he observed, the French Revolution owed a great deal to English and especially American thinkers. Voltaire, Montesquieu, and even Rousseau, until he changed his mind, were admirers of British and American liberties. John Locke was one of Voltaire's idols. O'Brien also points out the roles played by Lafayette and Thomas Jefferson, who was the U.S. ambassador in Paris during the revolution. Lafayette, as the hero of the American Revolution, was the first to propose a Declaration to the French Assembly, and the revolutionary thinkers visited Jefferson's ambassadorial residence to solicit his advice.

In O'Brien's account, the French ended up forsaking the moderating influences of Locke, Lafayette, and Jefferson and opted for a kind of statist absolutism instead. Borrowing from Spinoza's idea of the secular state as an embodiment of the general will, or common good, Rousseau wrote his *Social Contract* in 1762. It was an attempt to devise a blueprint for a society where the sovereign people were as equal and free as in the state of nature, while abiding by the laws that expressed the general will. The substance of this general will, which was supposed to be infallible, like the most despotic Catholic popes, was not entirely clear. It would have to involve some form of religion, a "civil religion," in Rousseau's words, that transcended individual interests and bound the citizens together. Rousseau, unlike some of his radical predecessors but like Locke, and indeed Tocqueville, believed that when people have to cooperate, they need a common faith, albeit not one derived from the authority of a church. And the general will would have to be imposed. Rousseau: "In order then that the social compact may not be an empty formula, it tacitly includes the undertaking, which alone can give force to the rest, that whoever refuses to obey the general will shall be compelled to do so by the whole body."[22]

This idea was incorporated in a much harsher form by Rousseau's disciple, Abbé Sieyès, into the Declaration of the Rights of Man and of the Citizen. The nation was fetishized as the embodiment of the general will: "The nation exists before all, it is the origin of everything. Its will is always legal, it is the law itself."[23] Article 3 of the Declaration stipulated: "The source of all sovereignty resides essentially in the nation: no group, no individual may exercise authority not emanating expressly therefrom." This idea would lend itself not only to chauvinism but also to a new form of ideological oppression. For the power of whoever represented the nation, as the embodiment of the general will, was hard to challenge. To dissent from the will of the people was to be an enemy, or a traitor. That is how Robespierre saw the enemies of the people: "Our will is the general will." It was as if the rebels against absolute monarchy and the Catholic Church had replaced one kind of absolutism with another.

This is a price that is often paid when tyrannies are overthrown by zealots. Spinoza rightly detected this in the English revolution of the 1640s. As O'Brien says: "Robespierre's relation to the general will is precisely that of Cromwell to God."[24] The "enthusiasm" with which priests and nuns were hanged and churches burned by the French revolutionaries (or, much later, leftist republicans in the Spanish Civil War) showed the zealotry to which people can be driven by too many years of oppressive dogmatism.

Outside France, even thinkers who had been sympathetic to the revolutionary cause were shocked by the violence. Some ended up seeing the French Revolution as a tragedy. The chaos of France was a great spur for British conservatism. Lord Acton, a liberal Catholic in the mold of Tocqueville, declared that the French Revolution threw away the hope of freedom because of the passion for equality. Equality, in conservative British thinking, was equated with coercion.

Edmund Burke argued, like Hume, that the destruction of traditional institutions is always followed by something worse. Hence the desire for stability, including the stability that hierarchies bring. One does not have to be a passionate believer in God to wish for the preservation of

the Anglican Church, or a passionate devotee of monarchy to strive for its continuation. In fact, passion is to be
distrusted. It is precisely to contain the lethal passions of
man that tradition is needed. When British thinkers denounced the French Revolution for its godlessness, they
did not do so as religious fanatics but as traditionalists who
equated British liberties with ancient customs, from King
Alfred's Constitution to the rites of the Church of England.
Their problem was not with liberty; indeed, they argued
that the God-fearing British, who accepted that inequality was part of the human condition, were freer than the
godless French *citoyens* who were forced to conform to a
blueprint for a democratic utopia.

British conservatives had a peculiar ally of sorts in one
of the most ferocious French authoritarians thrown up by
the Enlightenment: Joseph de Maistre. A minor aristocrat
from the south and a Jesuit by education, Maistre was a liberal of sorts until the revolution and its aftermath changed
his mind radically. Revolution now struck him as God's
punishment for the hubris of man. Not an especially pious
figure, he still exalted the Catholic Church because of its
divine authority and its dogmatism. He pined for the return of absolute monarchy and believed that only the most
punitive justice could suppress the evil nature of man.

Rationalism, science, equality, natural rights, democracy, liberalism—these were all loathsome concepts to
him. He was a leading light of the counter-Enlightenment,
but not because of some Romantic passion for mystery or
obscurantism. He was not a Romantic. He was a radical
pessimist. The Enlightenment, to him, would not bring
progress, liberty, or greater knowledge, but chaos, violence, and depravity. Man could not be left to his own de-
vices. That is why order had to be enforced by traditional
authority, prejudice, instinct, and the hangman. If men
decline, he wrote, "to recognize authority where it legiti-

mately lies—in the Church and the '*divinisé*' monarchy—they will fall under the yoke of the tyranny of the people, which is the worst of all."[25]

But Maistre made an odd exception for England. The English, he said, had an unwritten constitution, which was divinely inspired, as it were. Their constitution was not the product of rational thought but merely "felt," and thus for Maistre a more reliable source of authority than all the shallow and misguided institutions that rationalists put their trust in.

Burke and other British conservatives might easily have gone along with this, even though they didn't share Maistre's brutal authoritarianism or indeed his pessimism. Isaiah Berlin wrote about Maistre that temperamentally he resembled his enemies. Like the Jacobins, he was a destroyer, a hater, an extremist. The revolutionaries wished to demolish the old order, create a tabula rasa, and build a new social order from scratch. Maistre, in Berlin's words, "was the polar opposite of this. He attacked eighteenth-century rationalism with the intolerance and the passion, the power and the gusto, of the great revolutionaries themselves."[26]

The difference between France and Britain, or indeed the United States, is the role of the Catholic Church. As Tocqueville pointed out, European unbelievers attacked the church more as a political than a religious enemy. He was certainly right about France. The Catholic Church was an extremely powerful political institution, with vast wealth in land and treasure. The Vatican was a source of absolute truth, and the authority of priests was almost total. The despotic monarchy of France was intimately linked to the church, which is why the Jacobins had to destroy both. Even though Louis XVI was far from despotic, they needed to crush the monarchy and purge religion from the public realm to put the secular state out of the church's reach. And Maistre, followed by generations of Catholic reactionaries, bent on revenge for the defeat of 1789, longed to revive the authority of church and monarchy to restore the original order.

Thomas Jefferson did not have this problem: Catholics were a vulnerable minority in the United States. This would change in the nineteenth century when new immigrants from Ireland, Italy, and Germany made the Roman church into the largest single Christian denomination and inspired considerable hostility. Only when Protestant hostility to Catholics more or less disappeared could the United States truly be called a country of religious tolerance. But that was in the twentieth century. In the early nineteenth century Tocqueville observed acutely that Catholics wanted all rights to be respected so that "they could be sure to enjoy their own in freedom." That is why they were led, "perhaps in spite of themselves, toward political doctrines which, maybe, they would adopt with less zeal were they rich and predominant."[27]

Jefferson did, of course, follow the French model in pushing religion out of the public sphere. As he said about Pennsylvania and New York, two states without established churches: "They have made the happy discovery, that the way to silence religious disputes, is to take no notice of them." But he did so not as an enemy of religion. He felt no need to destroy the churches, for none had anything like the power enjoyed by the Catholic Church under the ancien régime in France. On the contrary, he believed that separation of church and state would benefit religion.

On this issue, Jefferson was unwilling to compromise. But in his politics, he was not at all a radical. His ideal was a stable rural society of educated farmers disposed to democracy, because they were responsible for the land they owned. Although by no means a promoter of slavery, he did own slaves himself. And democracy, in his mind, was not really compatible with an industrial society, where large numbers of manual workers lived in huge, "pestilential" cities. He prized independence, which went together with ownership, and distrusted too much government. He wrote in his autobiography: "It is not by the consolidation, or concentration of powers, but by their distribution that good government is effected." And: "The purpose of establishing different houses of legislation is to introduce the influence of different interests or different principles."[28]

This could not be further removed from the Jacobin idea of the state as the embodiment of the people's will. But even on the religious front, Jefferson's notion of the secular state, strictly neutral in all religious matters, would soon be challenged by Christians who had a very different idea of the state. Already in the presidential campaign of 1800, Christian believers were accusing Jefferson of being an atheist and thus unfit to be president. Since Christians live "under the law of Christ," intoned John Mitchell Mason, a Presbyterian minister from New York, they should speak out against the falsehoods of party politics.[29] People like Mason continue to argue that the United States is a Christian nation and that the state has the duty to uphold Christian morals, in terms of family life, sexual practices, or the teaching of biology.

Yet they, too, are unlike their French counterparts, for their belief in American democracy, and the uniqueness of American freedoms, stands in stark contrast to the revanchist politics of Maistre, Charles Maurras, founder of the extreme right-wing Action Française, or Marshal Pétain, all of whom viewed democracy, and particularly the United States, with the deepest suspicion. American Christians of the Right may not be liberals and may even be bigots, but they still profess to believe in democracy.

They believe, as much as atheists, in the American civil religion, the difference being their conviction that freedom was bestowed on His chosen land by God.

Civil religion is a product of the democratic revolutions, both in the United States and France. What they have in common is their claim to a universal validity, like Christianity, or indeed Islam. The Napoleonic conquests, no less than the American idea of manifest destiny, were justified by the universalist claim. French republicanism, in the minds of its promoters, with its rationalist ideals of liberty, equality, and fraternity, could and indeed should be applied everywhere. In the American case, the secularist idealism of the founding fathers has been complicated by the assertion among Christian believers that the nation's destiny is guided by higher powers.

Since such metaphysical assertions can still be heard in the United States today, Europeans are inclined to agree with the American essentialists that they reflect a uniquely American phenomenon. This, too, however, is an error. Similar claims have been made by Protestants in other Western democracies, including or indeed especially in Spinoza's native country, the Netherlands. The politics of the great Dutch statesman Abraham Kuyper (1837–1920) was but one example of an attempt all over Europe in the mid-nineteenth century to claw back European politics from Enlightenment liberalism. As an orthodox Calvinist, he was hostile to the Catholic Church. His idea of the true Dutch nation was soundly Protestant, an identity forged in the eighty-year revolt against the Spanish king. But he was entirely sympathetic to Pius IX's all-out attack on godless rationalism and liberalism. His political party, which he led for many years as a cabinet minister and prime minister, was called the Anti-Revolutionary Party.

The revolution it opposed was of course the French one. Kuyper rather admired the American Revolution and was a follower of Burke. But his admiration did not really take into account Jefferson's Enlightenment ideals. What he liked especially about the United States was its Protestant religiosity and the peaceful nature of its democratic institutions. He shared Burke's hostility to the French Revolution, even though Burke's traditionalist view of the Anglican Church was liberal compared to Kuyper's Calvinist orthodoxy.

In some ways, Kuyper was very much like his populist Christian American counterparts. His distrust of the liberal, educated elite was such that he did not consider them to be part of the Dutch *volk*. The spirit of Erasmus, Grotius, and Spinoza, in his view, had alienated the Dutch from their Christian roots. Those "deniers of Christ," those "self-satisfied thinkers," may be more learned than the common believer, whom Kuyper championed, but they were divorced from "the stream of national life."[30] This is also why he distrusted central government run by city slickers. The real *volk* lived in small towns. The true national culture was provincial. What Kuyper's Anti-Revolutionaries aimed at was to re-Christianize the nation, to return Dutch society to its orthodox Protestant roots. His archenemies, more than the Catholics, who were at least believers in God, were the liberals, who had dominated politics since the 1840s.

Also like the American Christians, and unlike the French anti-revolutionaries, he believed in democracy. He even believed in the separation of church and state. Indeed, he insisted on it, for the sake of the church. "Not a state church, but a church state" was his motto. There would be no established church, but everything from school education to national politics should reflect the Calvinist beliefs of the true Dutch people. Since he had to accept, with a certain reluctance, that Catholics, socialists, and liberals shared his nationality, it was impossible to impose his Christian vision on everyone. The solution was not to separate religious belief from political argument or ban religion from the public sphere but to divide the public sphere up into autonomous "pillars." This was designed to protect religion from the state. The orthodox Protestants would have their own schools, universities, sports clubs, newspapers, pension funds, and political parties, and so would the Catholics, the socialists, and the liberals. People would vote not according to their interests but their deepest beliefs, which were, in the case of pious Christians, held to be the same thing.

Kuyper's Anti-Revolutionary Party no longer exists. After the pillars were fatally undermined by the social changes of the 1960s, it merged with Catholic and other Christian parties to form the Christian Democrats. But his ideals live on. Apart from the Christian Democrats, there are still a number of political parties reflecting the views of more or less orthodox Protestant denominations. Faith-based education is still financed by the state. The Netherlands never did become a church state, as Kuyper had hoped, but even in these far more secular times religion still has a place in the public domain, unlike in France.

Europe and the United States, then, cannot be neatly divided into two distinct entities. It would be more accurate to see the relations between politics and faith in America as just another variation in a varied Western world, divided, as much as anything else, by the differences between Rome and the Protestant churches. In France, public secularism, or *laïcité*, is, as it were, an article of faith. The general will is represented by individual citizens. There is no room in the public sphere for organized religious belief. In England, the established Church of England, whose services fewer and fewer people attend, is part of the national culture, whose rituals, like those of the monarchy, are regarded with fondness, irritation, or indifference. Large-scale immigration since the 1960s has added some new members to the church, as well as enabling a variety of cultures rooted in the former empire to lay claim to part of the public space. In post-Reagan America, a newly organized Christian coalition has been mobilized to enter the political realm in a way that challenges the Jeffersonian state. In Germany and the Netherlands, Christian democracy survives in largely secular societies, whose values are being challenged not, for the moment, by Christian zealots but by the increased presence of Islam.

•   •   •

Political problems concerning religion in Europe and the United States *seem* so distinct that it is easy to miss the considerable differences among European nations. The rise of the Christian Right in the United States, as well as the various responses to Islam in Europe, reflect earlier social changes, especially those that came from the cultural turbulence of the 1960s. All have to do with the question of national identity, just as was true in the revolutionary 1790s, the anti-revolutionary 1860s, and the revolutionary 1930s. Religious, or indeed secularist, zealots like to fix or freeze collective identities in terms of revealed, unalterable orthodoxies about faith, culture, or race. In reality, who or what we think we are is always much more fluid.

In the 1960s, youth rebellion in Britain was largely about class and the national institutions designed to preserve a system based on it. It was also about debunking national myths. War heroes were mocked in satirical television programs, as were Anglican vicars and the queen. Since none of these symbolic figures was especially oppressive, the satire was, certainly in hindsight, mild, even affectionate. The vicar was a figure of fun, not hatefulness.

41

And many vicars saw the joke, pretending to be "with it" by affecting a liking for the Beatles and so on. Class was challenged by such pop icons as cockney photographers, irreverent television hosts, and rock stars who thickened or even adopted working-class accents and partied with the aristocracy.

As with all youth rebellions, sex played a large part. In the United States, sexual "liberation" was seen as a blow to religious morality. In Britain, again, class was more important. The trial surrounding the publication of D. H. Lawrence's *Lady Chatterley's Lover* is often thought to have kicked off the 1960s. As Philip Larkin wrote in his famous poem: "Sexual intercourse began / In nineteen sixty-three / (Which was rather late for me) / Between the end of the Chatterley ban / And the Beatles' first LP." What shocked British conservatives was not sodomy per se (a not uncommon practice, one presumes, in some of the better private schools) but the fact that it was performed by a common gardener on a lady.

The most famous satirical program on British television, *That Was the Week That Was*, was imitated on Dutch TV in the early 1960s. A mild sketch about the Dutch middle class worshiping their newly acquired TV sets by reciting the Lord's Prayer, substituting the word "TV" for Father, caused an uproar. Questions were asked in parliament. Newspaper editorials called for an instant ban. Hate mail hinted at Jewish plots. The participants received death threats. It showed that Dutch Protestantism could still be much fiercer than cozy Anglicanism. But the real challenge of 1960s culture was social, even political. For the revolt against traditional sexual morality and paternalistic "repressive tolerance" (Marcuse's much quoted term) was really against the pillars of society, the institutional power of churches, political parties, and educational establishments. The monarchy, too, came under fire, when

protesters in Amsterdam tried to disrupt the crown prin-
cess's wedding to a German diplomat by obscuring the
royal couple from public view with smoke bombs.

In France, it was the stifling atmosphere of Gaullist government, authoritarianism in French universities, and the
lingering influence of petit-bourgeois Catholic morals that
sparked the student riots in May 1968. "L'imagination au
pouvoir!" may sound like a romantic assault on French
rationalism, and in a way it was. But this being the land
of Robespierre, doctrinal battles were also more extreme
than in other parts of Europe. Maoism was taken up by
some Western intellectuals everywhere, but the French intelligentsia took to it with special zeal.

And then there was the history of World War II. British youths asserted themselves by making fun of war heroes, shocking to some older people, no doubt, but something of minor importance. In France, the pro-Catholic,
pro-Nazi, anti-Semitic legacy of the Vichy regime, ignored
by General de Gaulle in order to put a cracked nation together again, finally had to be confronted. German children blamed their parents for the Third Reich and vowed
to resist "fascism," violently if need be. Dutch youths
taunted the police by comparing Amsterdam cops to the
Gestapo and the SS.

In the United States, patriotism, especially the notion
of America's destiny to free the world by force of arms,
this time in Vietnam, was a major issue; hence the ostentatious flag burning on campuses and rock 'n' roll stages,
even as British rockers, in a gentler spirit of mockery,
wrapped themselves in the Union Jack. But the main thing
was race, and this was linked to sex, and, of course, this
being America, to religion. The rhetoric of Martin Luther
King owed a great deal to religious traditions, especially
the social gospel preaching of black Baptist churches, and
the teachings of Mahatma Gandhi. But he was also influ-

enced by Reinhold Niebuhr's criticisms of capitalism. King used the pulpit to say what young dropouts (mostly from the prosperous middle class) were also saying, in their countercultural ways: "Automobiles and subways, television and radios, dollars and cents, can never be substitutes for God."

King's social gospel was not just a product of the black churches but part of a tradition that had never quite gone away in America since the late nineteenth century, when the Baptist minister Walter Rauschenbusch, among others, preached against the evils of Gilded Age capitalist greed. His was the other Christian voice, which grew fainter over time, outgunned by louder voices preaching the gospel of wealth: Andrew Carnegie, John Rockefeller, and others. King, Abernathy, and their brothers in arms revived this tradition to promote equal democratic rights for black citizens. Andrew Young: "Ours was an evangelical freedom movement that identified salvation with not just one's personal relationship with God, but a new relationship between people black and white."[31] When this fine ideal ran into hard barriers of prejudice, often bolstered by references to the scriptures, especially in the South, some black activists turned to Islam for solace and a sense of self-respect.

One thing American and Western European rebellions of the 1960s have in common, however, is the perception of those who opposed them that they were a metropolitan, elitist attack on the values of the ordinary, small-town folks, rooted in the native soil, the "little people" championed by a long line of populists, fascists, and religious zealots, from Abraham Kuyper to, as it were, Elmer Gantry. Special riot police from the provinces were bused into Paris in 1968 to teach the big-city students a lesson. The Provos of Amsterdam, with their long hair and white jeans, were mainly a provocation to the provincials who had never liked Amsterdam anyway. Hippies, Yippies, and other counterculturalists were based in San Francisco, New York, Los Angeles, and the university towns. The man who shoots the hippie biker Billy (Dennis Hopper) at the end of *Easy Rider* is not a greedy capitalist but a God-fearing yokel in a pickup truck from the heart of Louisiana.

When the backlash against social change came, sooner in some countries than others, it came as a populist reaction against the elites. The elites in Europe are blamed for dismissing national feeling in the quest for European unity and for allowing too many immigrants, especially Muslims, to "swamp" the cities of France, Holland, Britain, Denmark, and Germany. For the first time since the 1960s, religion became a contentious issue again.

The fear of Islam, its intolerance, and its links with revolutionary violence have not yet provoked a Christian revival. Because Europeans have fought religious institutions for more than two hundred years in the name of freedom, a struggle for liberty against Muslim believers cannot be couched plausibly in religious terms. It would seem like a contradiction. For many secular Europeans, it is the strength of Muslim belief that causes anxiety, as though rational "Enlightenment values" and liberal democracy were under siege by irrational faith. There is, however, a curiously religious, even apocalyptic undertone in some of the anti-Muslim rhetoric, an accusation that secular Europeans are bound to lose an existential war because they no longer believe in values, have become decadent and nihilistic, and are indeed, in this respect, inferior to the Muslims who have the benefit of their faith. The fear is that Western democracy might collapse, not because of Islam but because of the Europeans' lack of faith in their own civilization and their consequent refusal to fight for its survival.

In the United States, the struggle for freedom and civil rights was fought in the name of God. And so is the counterrevolution, which began in the early 1970s when white

Southern Baptists, shocked by the emancipation of blacks, deserted the Democratic Party and scrambled to the safety of large suburban churches. The message they heard in these giant malls of worship was an increasingly fundamentalist one. American identity had to be reasserted and taken back from the hands of effete, godless, urban elites who had done their best to destroy it. A vital part of this American identity is the notion of being free—the freest people on earth, free from big government, free to carry guns, free from foreign attack. Freedom, religion, and America, in the eyes of the many fearful Christians, go together. We were at war with "terror," claimed the last Republican administration; if left to the secular liberals, this war would be lost, and the apocalypse will come.

The gulf between Europe and the United States, then, is not as wide as might be presumed. Similar fears haunt anxious minds. Our histories are not the same and we have different notions of who we are. But everywhere people are trying to cope with the confusions of a fast-changing world by reaching for fixed—and quite often newly made up—identities based on race, religion, or national culture. This attempt to freeze ourselves into place is a challenge to the liberal society. Anti-liberalism can be directed against the alleged threat of Islam or against secular liberals. What is feared in both cases is a loss of identity, of something to believe in, of common bonds, ethical, cultural, or religious, without which people are afraid of being cast out, alone, into the state of nature. It is the kind of fear that drove the early American settlers into prayer tents, where the Elmer Gantrys of their day preached fire and brimstone and raked in the cash.

TWO

ORIENTAL WISDOM

Matteo Ricci reached China in 1583. Dressed in mandarin robes of the finest silk, he and fellow Jesuit missionaries introduced the imperial court to astronomy, mathematics, and cartography, among other things. Teaching science to the Chinese as a way of converting them to the Christian faith was a remarkable enterprise with decidedly mixed results. Some were converted, but others, accustomed to thinking of China as the center of the world, regarded world maps that showed the fallacy of this idea as an insult. And back in Rome, there was a great deal of resistance to the Jesuit penchant for going native among the heathen upper classes, especially when Ricci published learned texts showing the antiquity and moral refinement of Chinese civilization. Ricci was especially interested in Confucian philosophy, and denounced Buddhism and Taoism as primitive cults. As far as ancestor rites were concerned, he decided that they were not religious but cultural and political traditions and thus permissible, even in the case of Christian converts. Not surprisingly, members of less refined Catholic orders protested, and accused the Jesuits of encouraging demon worship and idolatry.

Although priests in Rome argued endlessly over this issue of rites, it was a minor problem compared to a much greater challenge from China to Christian dogma. If Chinese civilization preceded Christendom, which clearly it did, and if the Chinese had developed a code of behavior that was at least as moral as, if not superior to, Christian morality, then the Christians were faced with an agonizing choice. Either Spinoza and his followers were correct in thinking that moral behavior was entirely possible without believing in divine revelation, or it had to be proven that the Chinese believed in God.

Naturally, despite their great worldly sophistication, Jesuits could not accept the first proposition, so they argued that the ancient Confucians had indeed believed in a supreme divine being but that faith in God had been corrupted by later schools of Chinese philosophy. Intellectual libertines and Spinozists, just as naturally, took the opposite view. Their Sinophilia focused on Chinese scientific discoveries and the supposedly Platonic nature of the Chinese state. The seventeenth-century Dutch scholar and librarian Isaac Vossius particularly admired a political system that allowed "philosophers and lovers of philosophy" to correct rulers' mistakes. Indeed, "were the rulers to err, the philosophers enjoy such great freedom to admonish those things as formerly was scarcely even found among the Israelite prophets."[1]

So, not quite a democracy, as we know it, but a more open system than what most Europeans had known at the time. The idealization of Confucianism by European radicals is especially interesting in the light of what future generations of Chinese would say. In the early twentieth century Chinese intellectuals would come to see Confucianism as the main obstacle to their twin modern ideals, which they called "Mr. Science" and "Mr. Democracy."

However, Vossius and others, such as the French thinkers Pierre Bayle and Henri de Boulainvilliers, were so taken by Confucian thought that they believed it should be universally applied. They identified Confucius directly with Spinoza.[2] Mankind would progress by studying the philosophies of both men. The Sinophiles of the early Enlightenment did not deny that the Chinese had some notion of a supreme power but argued that they, like Spinoza, identified this power with nature, which should be studied rather than worshiped. What was especially admirable about the Chinese, in the eyes of European philosophes, many of whom lived in aristocratic France, was the meritocratic nature of the state, whose officials were selected on intellectual merit, not the happenstance of birth.

Voltaire, now better known for his Sinophiliac writings than Vossius or Boulainvilliers, took something from the Jesuits and something from the Spinozists. He accorded to the Chinese a form of Deism and paid the same tribute to the Indians: "It is most probable the religion of India was for a long time the same as that of the Chinese government, and consisted only in the pure and simple worship of a Supreme Being, free from any superstition and fanaticism."[3]

This dubious assumption tells us more about Voltaire than the civilizations of which he had only scant knowledge—which is not to say that he thought all Chinese, or Indians, were rationalists. On the contrary, like Matteo Ricci, Voltaire had no time for popular beliefs. The common people, he said, "governed by bonzes, are as rascally as ours.... [T]hey have a thousand ridiculous prejudices, as we do ... [and] they believe in talismans and in judicial astrology, as we used to believe for a long time."[4] In a delicious thought experiment, Voltaire imagined how religious figures from all parts of the world would be judged in Heaven by a court of sages, including Confucius, Socrates, and Epictetus: "I saw troops of fakirs arriving right and left, Buddhist priests, white, black, and gray monks, who all imagined that in order to pay their court to the Supreme Being, they must either chant or scourge themselves, or walk stark naked. I heard a terrible voice ask them: 'What good did you do mankind?' This question was succeeded by a gloomy silence; no one dared to answer; presently they were all led off to the madhouse of the universe: that's one of the biggest buildings you can imagine."[5]

It was superior virtue that Voltaire admired, not faith. The Brahmin, he thought, unlike the corrupt Christian clergyman, was a perfect example of detachment and meditative living. In Voltaire's words: "There being so great a physical difference between us and the natives of India, there must undoubtedly have been as great a moral one. Their vices were in general less violent than ours."[6] This was pretty much how Voltaire saw Confucian mandarins too, and indeed how they saw themselves, as cultivated, moderate, reasonable, benevolent—anything but fanatic. Fanaticism, in Voltaire's view, "is to superstition what delirium is to fever and rage to anger."[7] All religions—Jewish, Christian, as well as Buddhist—were prone to this madness, but Voltaire had a special loathing for sectarian dogmas of the Christian church, which had caused such mayhem in Europe.

Although Confucius presented himself to his followers as a passionate man, he would not have disagreed with Voltaire's picture of the great Chinese sage's philosophy. Self-cultivation, moderation in all things, a critical spirit—all these were essential to the makeup of the Confucian gentleman (*junzi*). *Toujours pas de zèle* could have been Confucius's motto, even though it was Talleyrand who coined it. As far as the metaphysical world is concerned, we don't know exactly what he believed. When his disciple Zilu asked him how to serve the spirits and gods, Confucius replied: "You are not yet able to serve men, how could you serve the spirits?" When Zilu asked about death, the Master answered: "You don't yet know life, how could you know death."[8]

This passage has been interpreted as proof of Confucius's atheism. But this reading may well be false. All he was pointing out was Zilu's ignorance, not that spirits and gods didn't exist. The Sinologist Simon Leys, who translated it, believes that Confucius in fact regarded the Will of Heaven as "*the* supreme guide of his life," so much so that Confucius saw his work as a political consultant to various rulers as a heavenly mission to restore ethics to a morally corrupted civilization.

Be that as it may, the ethics he preached were secular in nature, concerning proper behavior of children and parents, and of the ruler and his subjects: benevolence, loyalty, filial piety, humanity, and so on. Moral codes had to be based on certain conventions, passed on from previous generations. A ruler had to be especially diligent about performing the proper "rites," ceremonial customs designed to preserve harmony in his realm. To this day, the Japanese emperor—still in the ancient Chinese tradition—performs a ritual planting of rice every year, for without harmony in nature, there can be no harmony in society either.

Leys argues that the actual meaning of *li*, or rites, corresponds less to rituals than to our idea of mores. These were more important to Confucius than laws. The observance of rituals, of traditional forms of proper behavior, is what holds a civilized society together. Laws are necessary to punish wrongdoers, but they cannot form a basis for civilized human discourse—that can only come from cultivation of virtue. In the *Analects*, Confucius is quoted as follows: "Lead [the people] by political maneuvers, restrain them with punishments: the people will become cunning and shameless. Lead them by virtue, restrain them with ritual: they will develop a sense of shame and a sense of participation."[9]

Leys observes that Montesquieu, author of *L'Esprit des lois*, held a similar view. Too much lawmaking is a sign of civilization breaking down. Religion is what keeps men on the straight and narrow. Tocqueville certainly would have agreed. He wrote in *Democracy in America* that, in general, "too much importance is attached to laws and too little to mores."[10] American democracy worked, he believed, because Christianity gave people a common sense of morality.

Spinoza would have disagreed. Since moral behavior is not of divine origin, and man in the state of nature is neither moral nor immoral but simply a lone animal trying to survive in the jungle, only laws can make people behave in a civilized fashion. Spinoza was not a Christian, of course, unlike Montesquieu, Tocqueville, or indeed Simon Leys. Then, nor was Confucius. Like Spinoza, he did not believe that man is born in sin—quite the opposite, in fact. He thought that man is born good, and society corrupts. This is where he differs from Spinoza, who was convinced that man is only capable of moral behavior in society. It is the duty of the Confucian official to rectify the moral corruption of society by polishing his own ethical behavior and criticizing the ruler if he strays from the path of virtue. "Government," he said, "is synonymous with righteousness. If the king is righteous, how could anyone dare be crooked?"[11]

Here again the Spinozists were wrong to identify their man too closely with the Chinese sage. For Spinoza did not believe you could rely on the virtue of a ruler. If you did that, you would soon find that the ruler would act out of self-interest and abuse his authority. Spinoza had grasped one of the most important principles of democracy in a way that Voltaire did not. But then Voltaire, although he was all for the freedom of thought, was no democrat. Nor did he have a deep interest in China or India per se. Like the Maoists and Ho Chi Minh enthusiasts in the West several centuries later, he used an idealized image of a faraway land to criticize conditions in his own country, which was still in the grips of an authoritarian church and an absolute monarchy. This is why he claimed that "the constitution of [the Chinese] empire is in fact the best in the world, the only one founded entirely on paternal power (which doesn't prevent the mandarins from caning their children); the only one in which the governor of a province is punished when he fails to win the acclamation of the people upon leaving office; the only one that has instituted prizes for virtue, while everywhere else the laws are restricted to punishing crime."[12]

Voltaire was right about one thing, which had already been observed by early Christian missionaries: Chinese civilization was both ancient and blessed with a code of ethics, which shaped the behavior of one of the most sophisticated bureaucratic systems known to man. But as many Chinese intellectuals have argued since the nineteenth century, the Confucian tradition might have been more of a hindrance than a help in the development of democratic rule.

•   •   •

A little less than a century after Voltaire wrote up his thoughts on China and India in the *Philosophical Dictionary*, China was devastated by a religious rebellion unleashed by a failed Confucian scholar named Hong Xiuquan. After his third failure to pass the examination that would have allowed him to become a scholar-official, Hong had a dream. In his dream he was handed a sword by an old man with a blond beard and instructed to slay evil spirits by a younger man, whom Hong addressed as "Elder Brother." Six years later, in 1843, when he failed to pass his exam for the fourth time, he read some Christian tracts that he had received from an American Protestant missionary in Canton. This sparked a revelation. The bearded man in his dream was clearly God, and his Elder Brother was none other than Jesus Christ.

An energetic and charismatic figure, driven by resentment against the Confucian establishment, Hong soon began to gather converts as an itinerant preacher. After studying the Bible with another American in Canton, he roamed round the wild southern province of Guangxi, converting thousands of people, many of them from the Hakka minority like himself. From Guangxi, Hong worked his way up through Hunan, where Mao Zedong's communist guerillas would operate with ferocious violence a hundred years later. The younger brother of Jesus set out to purge the lands of the moral depravity of the foreign Manchus, whose Qing Dynasty had poisoned China, in the view of Han nationalists, since they grabbed power in 1644. In fact, however, the rot had set in much earlier, according to Hong. Once, long ago, the Chinese had worshiped God, but their minds had been corrupted by Confucius and his followers. After striking out the Manchu demons, Hong promised to establish the Heavenly Kingdom of Great Peace (Taiping Tianguo). By 1849, he had 10,000 followers. In 1850 he had more than 20,000. A year later, it was 60,000. By the time the Heavenly Kingdom finally came into being in the southern capital of Nanjing, he had many millions of followers, ready to share their worldly goods, worship Christ, and renounce dancing, drinking, opium, and alcohol.

The purge of the unbelieving demons was a bloody affair. After the fall of Nanjing, 40,000 Manchu men, women, and children were burned, drowned, or put to the sword. Buddhist, Confucian, and Taoist temples were razed. And Jesus expressed his satisfaction in classical Chinese poems, passed down from Heaven to his younger brother Hong, now known as the Heavenly King, or Lord of Ten Thousand Years. Some of the goals of the Taiping were actually quite progressive. Social and economic equality was a primary goal. Land was distributed to families, according to their size. Women were given senior jobs in the administration and allowed to sit for examinations. Whether one can call the division of men and women in separate living quarters a progressive move is a moot point. It was certainly in line with the kind of puritanism encouraged by Christian movements all over the world.

But within a decade things began to unravel as they usually do in godly kingdoms on earth. A rival, named Yang Xiuqing, claimed that he was the Holy Ghost, thus senior to Christ's younger brother. And the Heavenly King began to behave in the manner of decadent Chinese rulers before and indeed after him. More and more remote from his people, pampered by a harem of concubines (even as his subjects were clubbed to death on the merest suspicion of adultery), he obsessively combed the Bible for references to his sacred mission in China.[13]

When the Qing armies, supported by Western powers, who did not like the Taiping attitudes to trade nor their version of the Christian faith, finally laid siege to Nanjing in 1864, it did not take long for the Heavenly Kingdom to come crashing down. The people starved, even as their king promised that God would drop manna from Heaven. The king himself died, ostensibly to join his elder brother. God's help failed to materialize. And those who survived the famine were massacred, some of them drowned in sewage flooding the tunnels the Qing troops had dug under the city walls. Once order was restored, as many as thirty million people had died as a consequence of a failed Confucian scholar's religious dream.

If Voltaire had been alive, the terrible story of the Taiping would doubtless have confirmed his dim view of Christianity. Here was proof, if ever it was needed, of the destructive forces unleashed by monotheistic dogma.

Would he have been right?

That Christian hysteria can be murderous is hardly news. But in this case, an older current of violent millenarianism ran under the veneer of Christianity, which appears and reappears throughout Chinese history whenever the powers of an imperial dynasty wane. The Taipings were a dramatic symptom of the Qing Dynasty's weakness. When Hong had his first intimations of divinity, China was being humiliated by British gunships in the Opium Wars. The common fate of feeble rulers in China is to be overthrown by men who promise to purge the world of moral corruption and rebuild Heaven on earth.

If rebellion usually had a religious component in China, so did imperial rule. The story of the founding emperor of imperial China, Qin Shi Huang, literally the First Emperor, would have bolstered Voltaire's claim for the superior wisdom of Confucianism even further. For the First Emperor, who conquered several kingdoms to establish a Chinese Empire in 221 BC, who standardized Chinese script as well as weights and measures, and who built the beginnings of the Great Wall, was a pitiless enemy of the Confucian scholars and their traditional mores.

Since Chinese history was written by Confucian scholars, accounts of the First Emperor's wickedness are bound to be exaggerated. We do not know all that much about him. But he *did* exist, China *was* unified, and we know that Legalism was the philosophical foundation of his rule. The emperor and his chief adviser, Li Si, sought to control the population through a punitive legal code meant to inspire terror rather than respect. The many grand projects embarked on during Qin Shi Huang's rule, which lasted until 210 BC, such as roads, canals, dams, and of course the Great Wall, were the result of mass mobilization and military discipline imposed by harsh punishments for any infringements of the laws.

From what little we know, the First Emperor aspired to be not just a worldly despot but also a master of the spiritual realm. If nature was divine, something ancient Chinese, including the emperor himself, almost certainly believed, he tried to conquer it, not just by damming great rivers but by quite literally stamping the landscape with written Chinese characters, as though claiming the ownership of a vast work of art by adorning it with his imperial seal. The written character is the chief symbol of Chinese civilization, which is why Chinese (as well as Japanese and Korean) rulers still like to display their calligraphy in public places, to show that civilization is in good hands. Inscribing mountain slopes and other places of natural beauty with official slogans—a habit that persists to this day—is a demonstration that all under Heaven is under the ruler's control. And all under Heaven meant Chinese civilization, or civilization *tout court*. The Great Wall, originally built to keep the northern nomads from encroaching on the empire, came in time to have a more symbolic function as the barrier separating the civilized from the barbarians.

The emperor's full title was Huangdi. Di is actually an ancient term for a divinity, or supreme being. Like Napoleon crowning himself in the presence of the pope or Nero declaring his own divine status, adopting this title was a way for the First Emperor to appropriate any form of spiritual or mystical authority that might be used against him. As is often the case with despotic rulers, the emperor became obsessed with his mortality, searching for elixirs to live forever. Necromancers, foolish enough to foresee his end, were murdered. Even nature itself was punished for natural disasters that might be construed as ill omens. The emperor, according to legend, once had a mountain destroyed after a devastating storm blew from its wintry peak. The emperor's death finally came as the result of swallowing mercury pills, which were believed to make him immortal but in fact speeded his death. Worried that the announcement of the ruler's mortality might create chaos and confusion in the empire, the imperial corpse was kept in a carriage by his courtiers, who tried to disguise the smell of putrefaction by hitching it to two wagons filled with rotten fish.

Confucius, who died more than two hundred years earlier, would surely have deplored the First Emperor's hubris. Legalism was the antithesis of his thinking. This is why the emperor banned the Confucian classics and, again according to legend, had the heads of Confucian scholars lopped off after burying them up to their necks. He saw them as a threat, precisely because they put traditional mores above the letter of the law. They "used the past to criticize the present," which was taken as a direct challenge to the legitimacy of his rule. For this he was, quite understandably, denounced as a frightful tyrant by generations of Chinese historians.

The First Emperor's reputation only changed for the better in relatively recent times. Mao Zedong, who also loathed Confucianism, and indeed all intellectuals who used the past to criticize the present, rather admired the First Emperor, as indeed he admired the Heavenly King of the Taiping. The latter, in his view (as well as that of Karl Marx), was a great rebel hero and the former a great unifier. Mao, in his own eyes, and those of his admirers, was both. After hounding many men to their deaths in one of his bloody purges, Mao once said: "[The First Emperor] buried 460 scholars alive; we have buried forty-six thousand scholars alive.... You [intellectuals] revile us for being Qin Shi Huangs. You are wrong. We have surpassed Qin Shi Huang a hundredfold."[14]

Neither Legalism nor millenarianism, then, can be said to have been conducive to liberal rule, let alone anything resembling democracy. Confucianism, at its best, was certainly more moderate. Whatever later generations of Confucian philosophers made of the Master's words, Confucius himself held that government, to be successful, had to be based on popular consent. Even though Confucius, like so many great figures in Chinese history, was eventually venerated as a deity, he was a thoroughly secular figure during his lifetime. And yet, when it comes to the influence of metaphysics in political affairs, the case for Confucianism is not so straightforward. Modern Chinese critics of Confucianism, who saw it as an ideological barrier to "Mr. Democracy," may have had a point.

In the Chinese tradition, harmony of the universe and harmony of society, politics, and cosmology are inseparable. Hence, the importance of omens and natural phenomena but also rites. Since the Chinese ruler was given the mandate of Heaven to be the custodian of cosmic as well as social harmony, he was the source of spiritual as well as secular authority. It was the duty of the Confucian mandarins to protect his authority by imposing their moral ideology on society. They were the guardians of the ruler's virtue and the "priests," as it were, of the official dogma that gave legitimacy to the state.

Confucius, and later Mencius, conceded that the people had the right to rebel against rulers who no longer provided them with social order or an adequate supply of food. If disharmony ruled, the mandate of Heaven would be withdrawn. But since politics, morality, and cosmology were so closely linked, political transformations would normally be couched in spiritual and moral terms. In this sense, millenarian rebels, such as the Taiping, lived in the same mental universe as the Confucianists. If society is held together by moral virtue and the Will of Heaven, and not by social contract or law, then any rebellion has to be seen as an attempt to restore virtue and appease Heaven.

Until monarchs were divested of their divine rights, more or less the same might be said about European politics, too. And the relative importance of shared ethics and the rule of law in modern democracies is still a matter of debate in Europe no less than Asia. The question is whether the split between spiritual and secular authority, which occurred in Europe, ever took place in China.

In theory this should have happened when China had its revolution in 1911. The Qing Dynasty was brought down, ending more than two thousand years of imperial history, and the Chinese Republic was founded. This followed decades of reforms, rebellions, and harsh crackdowns. In 1900, the Boxers United in Righteousness, or Boxers for short, a band of martial arts enthusiasts inspired by folk beliefs and popular stories about righteous rebels, tried to revive China's spirit by attacking foreign missionaries. One of their poetic effusions ran as follows:

> There are many Christian converts
> Who have lost their senses,
> They deceive our Emperor,
> Destroy the gods we worship,
> Pull down our temples and altars,
> Permit neither joss-sticks nor candles,
> Cast away tracts on ethics,
> And ignore reason.
> Don't you realize that
> Their aim is to engulf our country?"[15]

The Boxers were mostly rural folk who believed that spirits would make them invulnerable to bullets or swords. In the way the Boxers viewed China's decadence in moral or indeed spiritual terms, they were not just typical of previous insurgents but set the tone for rebellions to come. They were defeated by the foreign powers, who were perhaps less interested in saving missionaries and spreading the gospel than in protecting their commercial interests.

Even on a much higher intellectual plane, many late nineteenth-century Chinese reformers with liberal ideas were traditional moralists at heart. Kang Youwei, for example, was an extraordinary thinker who combined Confucian notions of humanism with socialist ideas on public welfare, state education, and female emancipation. Although he never shook off its influence, he rebelled against his Confucian education and wanted to destroy the traditional Chinese family. But he became most famous for his mystical vision of uniting mankind under one benevolent government. What was needed was not just a political change (he was in favor, at various times, of a constitutional monarchy and a communist state) but a spiritual transformation. Only then would China, and ultimately the world, rise to great heights again.

Sun Yat-sen, the father of the 1911 Revolution, picked up progressive ideas from his studies in Japan and the West and wanted to make China into a democracy, as he understood it. Like many people at the time, especially in East Asia, Sun was much taken by social Darwinism. In the struggle for survival, only the fittest races had a chance. The Chinese race, he believed, would take hold of its destiny by getting rid of the Manchus and building a democratic, socialist state. Even now, many Chinese still feel the humiliation of the late empire, when China was not only ruled by Manchus but was too weak to resist being exploited by Western imperialists. Sun wrote in 1906: "Our nation is the most populous, most ancient, and most civilized in the world, yet today we are a lost nation.... [O]ur ancestors did all they could for our prosperity; it is we, their descendents, who should feel ashamed."[16]

Apart from being a Darwinist, as well as a Chinese patriot, Sun was also a Christian. In a speech to Chinese Christians in Beijing, he said: "Several years ago, when I first advocated a revolution and began working and agitating for one, I knew that the essence of such a revolution could be found largely in the teachings of the Church. Today, it is the Church, not my efforts, that is responsible for the Republic of China."[17]

Of course he knew to whom he was speaking. Few Chinese would have taken this view. But in the sense that he saw the revolution in moral, even religious, terms, he was not only speaking his own mind but also conforming to a familiar Chinese pattern. Many Christians around the world would have shared his idea of politics, of course, but Chinese Christians, especially those of Sun's generation, bore the imprint of two traditions: their Christian ethics were grafted onto a Confucian view of the world, and especially of their own society as a moral universe whose harmony, based not on laws or contracts but on moral ideals, should mirror the harmony of Heaven.

The May 4 Movement of 1919 was not on the face of it a religious enterprise. It was sparked by the Treaty of Versailles, which concluded World War I. The Chinese government was unable to prevent the Western powers from handing over German concessions in China to Japan, a belated and largely passive participant in the Great War. To Beijing University students and a number of patriotic intellectuals, this was a sure sign that the government was too corrupt, weak, and cowardly to safeguard the nation's interests. So they called for a national revival, a political, moral, and cultural housecleaning. The cobwebs of the past, especially Confucianism, should be swept away, and "Mr. Science" and "Mr. Democracy" would rule. Indeed, the whole idea of what it meant to be Chinese needed rethinking. Lu Xun, the leading writer of the movement, observed that the 1911 Revolution had failed to change the Chinese character. What was at stake was not just politics but civilization itself.

Since Chinese civilization is symbolized by the written word, the Chinese language became a central topic of debate. One of the most striking figures at the time was Chen Duxiu, who argued for the abolition of classical Chinese as an elitist expression of outmoded ideas. He, too, was a moralist, in a Darwinist but also a quasi-Confucian way. The Chinese people would be "eliminated in the process of natural selection," he said, if they were unable to cultivate their individual characters.[18] Chen became one of the first members of the Chinese Communist Party in 1920.

"May 4," in fact, represented many things. It promoted an almost blind faith in science. Democratic change was called for, as well as a new Chinese prose style. The word "new" popped up as a mantra in pamphlets, slogans, books, and periodicals. What was not new, however, was the all-encompassing ambition of the movement, the ideal of a born-again, unified China. Not all who participated were Marxists. Some were liberals, followers of John Dewey, Bertrand Russell, or Herbert Spencer. But Marxism lent itself well to a people in motion, especially the bookish Chinese. It was "scientific," modern, anti-capitalist, egalitarian, and theoretical. It also had a unifying dogma to replace Confucianism. It promised the birth of a new morality, a new man, a new China. What was still lacking was an emperor, blessed with a mandate from Heaven. Chen Duxiu was unable to take on that role. Mao Zedong did instead, which is why Chen was written out of the history books, for the divine chairman brooked no rivals.

•   •   •

Mao unified China and imposed a harsh new order, in the manner of the First Emperor. For this he is still venerated by many Chinese. Some traditionalists even worship him as a folk god, whose golden image dangles from many a rearview mirror in Chinese taxis.

In some respects Mao's rule was a caricature of the worst aspects of traditional Chinese politics. He borrowed from the Legalists a system of draconian punishments for the merest hints of dissent. The cult of the Little Red Book was a grotesque echo of the dogmatism of Confucian ideologues. The enforced veneration of Mao's words, especially his calligraphy, turned the respect for the written word in Chinese civilization into a cult of the ruler himself. He was worshiped as a god, especially during the Cultural Revolution, when the simple act of crumpling up a newspaper bearing his image could lead to a death sentence. If ever there was a case of religious and secular authority being one and the same, Maoism was it. As in the Soviet Union under Stalin, or Hitler's Germany, this proved the danger of forcing people to renounce all religious beliefs and to worship a worldly leader instead.

Still, Mao was right to fear that charismatic rule cannot last. It never did in Chinese history. The messianic founders of new dynasties, who came to power through millenarian rebellions, were followed by weaker men who let the mandarins run the empire while they withdrew into their palaces to write elegant poems or play with their concubines. (Mao also conformed to this pattern for extended periods, only to reemerge as a ferocious tyrant.) Mao was followed by Deng Xiaoping, an able and sometimes ruthless leader who did not aspire to a cult of his person. And then came a succession of bureaucrats who still have their calligraphy, as well as their scholarly works (written by other bureaucrats), published to show that they are civilized men. They are far from being gods.

To most Chinese, the demise of charismatic rule must have come as a great relief. As a quasi-religious political ideology, Maoism is dead. But this loss, as well as the thorough destruction of older traditions, has left China with what many Chinese describe as a "spiritual vacuum." There is nothing left to believe in, except the famous slogan of Deng Xiaoping that "to get rich is glorious." Halfhearted attempts by the Communist Party to attach a higher meaning (and legitimacy) to its monopoly on power by resurrecting communist slogans and campaigns from the past are, on the whole, met with indifference and contempt.

What is not dead, however, in official circles, is the notion that secular power must be justified by a moral ideology, a kind of official state cult. The ideology currently being revived under the auspices of the Communist Party of China is, perhaps faute de mieux, none other than Confucianism—this after years of official denunciation of the ancient sage. What is stressed, however, is not the idea of the right to rebel against unjust rulers but the late neo-Confucian idea of absolute obedience to authority, a version of Confucianism that is consciously anti-democratic.

Contemporary China, in fact, is not at all devoid of spirituality. New cults, old folk beliefs, various forms of Christianity, some legal, some not, and Buddhist and Taoist sects, as well as all kinds of meditation and faith-healing groups, have sprung up like mushrooms after a rainstorm. The fact that Chinese citizens are not able to participate in politics, except in a very limited way in village elections, has made religion all the more popular. It is their only escape from pure materialism. Like imperial governments in the past, the communist government tries its best to keep all religious activity under its control. The Falungong, for example, a faith-healing, millenarian cult started by a charismatic meditation teacher, especially popular among elderly party cadres, seems harmless enough. But the government knows that it was precisely such cults that spread into rebellious movements in the past. And so it was crushed, in China at any rate.

Even if one does not condone the government ban, let alone its cruel persecution of Falun Gong supporters, it is doubtful that political movements emanating from charismatic groups would offer the quickest route to a democratic transformation. They are more likely to result in yet another cycle of Chinese history, of millenarian hope, followed by oppression.

Many Chinese Christians continue to argue, like Sun Yat-sen, that Christianity, with its stress on equality, charity, and duty to others, is the logical basis for democratic change. Some Christians even believe that China will be a democracy only once all Chinese have been converted to the Christian faith. It seems a dubious claim. To be sure, organized religion can assume a moral authority, to be mobilized against the authority of the state. This is particularly potent in a civilization where political authorities have traditionally sought to monopolize moral authority. But another religious revolt is hardly what China needs.

If democratic change is to come to China, it would have to involve a split between religious authority and secular rule. One must be allowed to exist independently of the other. No religion, not Buddhism, Taoism, Christianity, or the moral belief in Confucian ethics, need stand in the way of Chinese democracy. It has not done so in Taiwan. Confucian ethics, in the sense of benevolence, loyalty, and self-restraint, could even be a help. But this means that the political masters of the Chinese republic must renounce their authoritarian claims on the moral and spiritual lives of its citizens. Much has already changed since the death of Mao, but in this respect the rulers of the one-party state are as traditional as the long line of emperors and Confucian mandarins that preceded them.

•   •   •

Japan is a democracy, flawed, like all democracies, but a country with a free press, independent judges, and the right of all citizens to vote. Japanese like to claim that religion, in contrast to the Western world, plays only a minor role in Japanese life. What they mean is that Buddhism and Shinto, the majority religions in Japan, lack the dogmatic force of Christianity or Islam. Shinto, an amalgamation of nature-related rituals, does not have sacred texts of divine revelation. Most Japanese, when they marry or bury their kin, will pay deference to Buddhist or Shinto ceremonies, but that is often as far as religious practices go. Yet the claim that religion plays no part in Japanese politics would be wrong. One of the main contemporary political parties is tied to a Buddhist sect, and a political form of Shinto helped crush democratic aspirations in the past. Religion certainly played an important role in Japan's response to superior Western might.

Japan had a comparative advantage over the Chinese Empire when both were confronted with Western aggression in the middle of the nineteenth century. This was a matter of geography, as well as attitude, and the two were linked. Located on the farthest edge of the Asian continent—from the Western point of view, at any rate—Japan was spared the traumas of European colonial expansion. Also, Japan's peripheral perspective did not allow Japanese the luxury of thinking that they inhabited the center of the world. At least since the seventh century, and probably before, Japanese were well aware that the dominant civilization lay overseas.

This meant that Japanese had more time than other Asians to prepare for the Western waves that would sooner or later hit their rocky shores. After welcoming them at first, in the sixteenth century, the samurai government had little trouble cracking down on Catholic missionaries, as well as their Japanese converts, when they seemed to pose a threat to the political status quo. Once the Portuguese missionaries had been disposed of, Dutch traders, who had no interest in spreading God's word, could be safely contained in Deshima, a cramped little island off the port of Nagasaki, when Japan closed its borders to further European visitors for more than two hundred years.

But even in relative isolation, Japanese had a curiosity about other countries that often goes with the fear of provinciality, of being left out on the fringes. In this respect, too, they were not at all like the Chinese. By the time the Chinese Empire was humiliated in the Opium Wars, educated Japanese knew that China was no longer the great power it had once been. For the Chinese to adapt to the new world, where the balance of power had shifted so far in favor of the West, they would have to go through a cosmic change, as it were, upsetting the core of what it meant to be Chinese. The Japanese, on the margin of Chinese civilization, could simply look for the center elsewhere.

Largely through the heroic efforts of "Dutch scholars," who learned to read medical, scientific, and geographical texts in the Dutch language, Japanese knew more about the West than most Asians. One such scholar, reading a biography of Napoleon in Dutch, was so taken by the word for freedom, *Vrijheit*, that he softly intoned it whenever he got drunk.

The other factor that stood in the way of change in China was the concentration of power in the imperial government. Modernizing China called for a revolution, which again was more than a political shift. Bringing the imperial system to an end involved a breakdown of all the traditional institutions that gave legitimacy to political rule in China. There were reformists, such as Kang Youwei, who advocated a more moderate solution, hoping to paper over the transition with a constitutional monarchy. But they never had a chance. Once the Qing Dynasty broke down, without a new emperor to take over the dragon throne, it was like pulling a thread from a tattered old scarf; the whole system, with all its philosophical and religious underpinnings, came apart.

Again, Japan had a comparative advantage. After Prince Shotoku, patron of Buddhism in Japan, installed a Chinese-style political system in the seventh century, power was concentrated in the imperial court for several hundred years. But the authority of the court, located in Kyoto, was gradually eroded by regional samurai warlords and Buddhist clergy. By the twelfth century, after many bloody conflicts, the most powerful warrior clan established a government by shoguns, military strongmen, who left most cultural and religious duties to the emperors in Kyoto but kept worldly power for themselves. The most successful warrior clan of all, the Tokugawas, who ruled Japan between 1603 and 1867, further weakened the imperial court by shifting the base of political power to Edo, present-day Tokyo.

But even the authority of the Tokugawa shoguns was far from absolute. They still had to contend with regional samurai lords, whose relations with Edo were a matter of negotiation. Buddhist orders, especially Nichiren, also tried to protect their autonomy from the state, ultimately without success. And the imperial court, though much diminished, still had to be respected, if only because it was the emperor's blessing that gave legitimacy to the military rulers.

What this meant, in effect, was that Japan had fashioned a kind of separation between religious and worldly authority. The emperor became a revered spiritual figure, in charge of rites and ceremonies, while the shogun represented secular power. This arrangement was not entirely straightforward, in that the founder of the Junta, Tokugawa Ieyasu, was buried in a lavish temple complex north of Edo and was given divine status, like the Roman emperors.

Still, the separation of powers made it easier for Japan to make the necessary changes in the late nineteenth century to modernize the country and stave off foreign predators. There had already been sporadic uprisings in the countryside advocating the revival of imperial authority. As in China, such rebellions had a strong religious tinge. They never had a hope of succeeding until the 1850s, when the arrival of the American "black ships," commanded by Commodore Matthew C. Perry and armed with fearsome cannon, made the Tokugawa shogunate look tired, feeble, and clueless, rather like the Qing court during the Opium Wars. As a result, Japan, too, had a revolution of sorts, but not one that did away with the entire system and all its cultural underpinnings. Instead, provincial samurai, backed by city merchants, toppled the Tokugawa shogun and "restored" the emperor as the central ruler of Japan. They used a highly traditional institution to make a political revolution look like a restoration, as though the new Japan, with its modern, Western-style armed forces, political parties, factories, and new bureaucratic and industrial elites, dressed in European clothes, were actually returning to a truer, older, more traditional society.

In truth, however, much of this tradition was not only invented, as was the case in nineteenth-century European monarchies as well, but inspired by Western models. The Meiji emperor in Tokyo was partly a godlike Japanese mikado, partly a Napoleonic figure on horseback, and partly a German-style Kaiser. Instead of fighting unwinnable wars against the Western powers, which is what the Chinese opted for, the nineteenth-century Japanese elite, nativists as well as reformists, decided to learn as much as they could from the powerful foreigners in order to stand up to them. This meant, in their pretty much unanimous view, that Japan had to acquire an empire of its own, in Taiwan, Korea, and Micronesia. It also meant that Japan needed a

Kaiser in modern military dress, as commander in chief (in name at least) of the army and navy, and it meant that Japan needed a state religion.

In 1825, a patriotic scholar named Aizawa Seishisai wrote a famous polemical tract titled *New Theses*. Since this was still more than a decade before the Opium Wars, and thirty years before the arrival of Commodore Perry, Aizawa's fear of Western power was ideological more than military. After analyzing the source of Western imperial might, he concluded that Christianity was the key. Western rulers were able to unify their nations and command loyalty from their citizens because they had Christianity as a state religion. Japan, he decided, needed a state religion of its own, that is, in his phrase, "unity between religion and government" (*saisei itchi*), personified by an imperial ruler. The state, he believed, was more than a collection of political institutions; it was a spiritual community, a *kokutai*, "national essence."[19]

Since Aizawa was a nativist who had shifted his cultural focus from the Asian continent to Japan as the new center of Asian civilization, Buddhism clearly would not do. "The practitioners of this doctrine," he wrote, "sought to transform our Divine Land into another India, to convert innocent subjects of our Middle Kingdom into followers of the Indian barbarians. When transformed by barbarism within, how can 'what is essential to a nation' (*kokutai*) remain intact?"[20]

Although even the Japanese nativists were still steeped in Confucian thinking, Confucianism, if it can be called a religion at all, was not adequate as a national faith for the Japanese *kokutai* either. But Japanese nationalists did praise the efficacy of Christianity in Confucian, or at least traditional Chinese, terms. Christianity in Europe (as opposed to the debased forms brought to Asia by missionaries) was, in the words of Yokoi Shonan (in 1856), "based

on the Will of Heaven; its main doctrines follow the rules
of ethical behavior.... [I]t is a religion that combines government and edification."[21]

What was needed, then, was a purely Japanese faith.
Shinto, or Way of the Gods, seemed best able to answer
this need. It was certainly Japanese. For the common
people, Shinto was actually not a religion, in the sense of
having a doctrine, but a set of ceremonies and rites, often regional in nature, to do with fertility, good harvests,
clement weather, and so on. Anything natural could be
sacred: rivers, rocks, Mount Fuji. But the way nineteenth-
century nationalists pressed Shinto into national service
was something new.

Part of the emperor's duties had always been to worship
Amaterasu, the Sun Goddess, as his divine ancestor. She
now became a Japanese equivalent to the Christian God.
(In the view of some thinkers, she also proved the superiority of Japanese science, since the Japanese had known
long before Copernicus that the earth revolved around the
sun.) And now the emperor, more than being a custodian
of tradition, in the way of his ancestors, became the divine
focus of an official cult, which was more or less a modern
invention, along with steamships, conscript armies, and a
new constitution.

In one sense, the Japanese, who had separated religious
and secular authority in the past, inaugurated their modern age by putting them together again. But this, too, was
not straightforward. The emperor's powers were subject
to a certain degree of ambiguity, and so was the use of
religion, including Shinto. Before the emperor bestowed
the constitution to his subjects on February 11, 1889, the
anniversary of the date on which Jinmu, Japan's mythi-
cal first emperor, was believed to have founded the imperial line, he informed the spirits of his imperial ancestors

of the event in the privacy of his palace shrine. But the
constitution, drafted by men who had a good grasp of
European laws, was a secular document that gave a privileged section of the population the right to vote. It also
guaranteed freedom of religion and did not purport to reflect any particular faith. Yet it mentioned the "unbroken
line" of the emperor's ancestry, going all the way back to
the Sun Goddess. In the Imperial Rescript on Education,
promulgated in the following year, loyalty to the heirs
of this unbroken line was presented as the very basis of
the *kokutai*.

This clearly showed an official bias toward Shinto. Yet
it was argued, often to the chagrin of Shinto priests, that
this in no way confused religious with secular affairs, since
Shintoist worship of the imperial bloodlines was not a matter of faith but a national custom—culture, that is, not religion. And so, when Japanese Christians were accused of
disloyalty to their nation because they worshiped a foreign
deity, this was done from a quasi-secular perspective. The
famous Christian thinker Uchimura Kanzo, for instance,
was harshly attacked for failing to bow in reverence to
the Imperial Rescript on Education and accused of *lèse
majesté*. "The meaning of the Rescript," wrote the philosopher Inoue Tetsujiro, "is nationalism. But Christianity
lacks nationalism." Worse, Christians "do not differentiate
between their ruler and the rulers of other countries and
hold what are tantamount to cosmic beliefs. For those reasons Christianity is fundamentally at odds with the spirit
of the Rescript."[22] In times of nationalistic fervor, Japanese
Christians were often forced to choose between their God
and the emperor. The wrong answer could lead to severe
punishment.

The emperor's constitutional status was also cloudy.
In line with Western modernity, he was a constitutional

monarch who should leave governing to his secular government. But Ito Hirobumi, one of the great Meiji period oligarchs, made it clear that because "imperial sovereignty is the cornerstone of our constitution, our system is not based on the European idea in force in some European countries of joint rule of the king and his people."[23] And in the Imperial Precepts to Soldiers and Sailors of 1882, it is made very clear that members of the armed forces owe their absolute loyalty to the emperor, as their commander in chief, who relies on his soldiers and sailors "as our Limbs." That is to say, their obedience to the emperor took precedence over loyalty toward any elected government. The imperial cult, then, undermined democratic aspirations, held by many Japanese, from the start.

The ambiguity of the emperor's constitutional role did not matter greatly as long as the leading figures of the Meiji Restoration of the 1860s, the so-called oligarchs, were alive to make the most important political decisions. Ito Hirobumi and his fellow restorationists, men from provincial samurai clans in southwest Japan, were the real powers behind the imperial throne and the partly elected government. Once the oligarchs were gone, however, no one was able to stop the military nationalists, State Shinto ideologues, and militant anti-liberals. It was only in the 1930s that religious emperor worship came fully into its own, and a "holy war" was unleashed on the Asian continent to protect the *kokutai* and "bring all corners of the world under one imperial roof."

Japan's imperial system, as it existed until 1945, had two effects, apart from justifying military conquest. First, it actively impeded the successful development of democratic institutions. The emperor and his courtiers were extremely conservative men, whose primary duty was to protect the imperial institution. Liberals and democrats were viewed with deep suspicion, and the court's strongest political alliances were with equally conservative bureaucrats and military officers. Anyone who could speak for the imperial will trumped politicians, who were merely elected by the people. Even though the emperor's constitutional status was vague, his sacred presence worked in favor of authoritarian politics.

Second, his presence made it difficult, if not impossible, for a secular dictator to grab power. Japan never had a Hitler, or even a Mussolini, for the supreme authority was still vested in the sacred throne. Wartime allied propaganda sometimes made General Tojo Hideki out to be a dictatorial figure. In fact, Tojo, although certainly a martinet, was no more than a prime minister who could be deposed (not by voters, to be sure, but by fellow autocrats), as he was in 1944, when his government was deemed a failure. After 1940, Japan did have a fascist-type party, the Imperial Rule Assistance Association, but it was not a success, and its founder, Prince Konoe Fumimaro, prime minister at the time, was far from being a dictator. Some Japanese militants, especially in the middle ranks of the army officer class, did dream of making Japan into a fascist state with the emperor as a real dictator, but when they staged a coup in 1936, the emperor demanded that it be put down—one of the few instances of his direct intervention.

The fact that imperial Japan lacked a fascist or Nazi strongman did not necessarily make it more benign. Emperor worship was promoted as part of a chauvinistic ideology that justified atrocities against lesser breeds, that is, people not descended from the gods. But some of Japan's most excessive wartime behavior was due less to cruel dictatorship than to a fuzzy chain of command in a political system that lacked accountability because the emperor was responsible for everything, and nothing. Anything could be perpetrated in his name, even as he remained as passive as a sacred idol gathering dust in the inner sanctum of a holy Shinto shrine.

•   •   •

To the Americans who occupied Japan after its defeat, emperor worship was a form of dangerous idolatry. One of the first measures taken by the allied occupation authorities, led by General Douglas MacArthur, a devout Christian, was to ban State Shinto and make the emperor renounce his divinity. Emperor Hirohito had a speech released to the Japanese press on the first day of 1946. It was a much rewritten version of a draft written by two scholars, an American and an Englishman. The emperor talked about returning to Emperor Meiji's Charter Oath, promising a certain degree of democracy, without mentioning the nineteenth-century emperor's sacred status. Nor did Hirohito deny that he was descended from the Sun Goddess. But he did say that he was not a "manifest deity." This impressed the Americans more than the Japanese, who had only the haziest idea of what was meant by manifest deity (*akitsumikami*). A *kami*, they would have understood. Nature is full of *kami*, or holy spirits. The point was his divine ancestry, something he never renounced.[24]

Nonetheless, after 1945, Shinto was no longer a state cult, and the emperor went at least halfway to becoming a real constitutional monarch. Of course, religion did not go away, especially in such hard and bewildering times as early postwar Japan. Instead it was privatized. Several women, declaring that the Sun Goddess spoke directly through them, started highly successful cults, mostly re-volving around themselves. Different Buddhist and Shinto-derived sects and associations, many of them banned un-der the militarist regime, sprang to life and gathered large numbers of believers. These years, just after the emperor's declaration that he was human, became known as "rush hour of the gods."

Most Japanese were happy with their secular democ-racy, which the Americans had helped them set up. Few mourned the demise of emperor worship or State Shinto. But a hard core of nationalists, lodged in the conservative Liberal Democratic Party, organized crime, and right-wing intellectual journals, could never forgive the Americans and their liberal Japanese allies for having destroyed the "spirit" of the Japanese people. Their rhetoric is a mixture of Confucianist conservatism, with its emphasis on moral education, and Japanese chauvinism, with its reverence for cultural purity and sacred bloodlines. One of the chief goals of the rightists is to rewrite the postwar constitution, drawn up by Americans, by abolishing the pacifist Article 9, in which Japan renounces its right to use military force, and by reinstating the emperor as a sacred figure.

Just as hunger for material prosperity in China replaced the fervor of Maoism, dark memories of wartime extrem-ism were pushed away in Japan by a state-led effort to ex-pand the nation's wealth. In the early 1960s, Prime Minis-ter Ikeda Hayato promised the Japanese that their incomes would be doubled. Within two decades the country had become so rich that people from all over the world sought to imitate "the Japan model." But this led to a common complaint—again, as in post-Maoist China—that Japanese were suffering from a spiritual and moral vacuum. Mate-rialism did not seem enough. Conservatives talked about restoring the nation's moral fiber by going back to prewar moral education, with strong doses of patriotism. But the same alleged vacuum also lent itself to private spiritual enterprises, which were not always peaceful.

A half-blind guru named Asahara Shoko, using a mishmash of Hindu and Buddhist language, promised his followers in the Aum Shinrikyo that they would establish a utopian superpower after the rotten, corrupt, empty Japanese system had collapsed from a devastating assault. As a first step, in 1995, his disciples dropped sarin gas in the Tokyo subway, killing a dozen people and injuring thousands. People were shocked to hear that many members of this sinister cult were highly educated scientists, disgusted with the spiritual vacuum in a technological, capitalist society.

The liberal answer to the discontents of modern prosperity is that each should find his or her own way to Jerusalem. It is not the task of a liberal democratic state to provide answers to the deeper questions about life, let alone impose metaphysical beliefs on its citizens. Japan, as well as Asian countries occupied by imperial Japanese soldiers, was devastated because the Japanese state had tried to do just that.

Religion can play a part in promoting ethical behavior, but it is not the only moral glue available to hold a society together. Locke and Tocqueville talked about the necessity of faith, but Spinoza spoke about the law, Hume about tradition, Confucius about rites, the fast vanishing Japanese Left about pacifism, and the still limited, but highly visible, Japanese Right about restoring the prewar national spirit.

This old spirit is hard to rekindle because it was so badly discredited by Japan's wartime record. Debates about World War II in Japan are still vexed for that reason. Pacifists use the past as a warning. Right-wing conservatives gloss over that same past to burnish the spiritual ideals that were tarnished by the war. Emperor worship was an experiment in mixing politics with religious faith, which destroyed the chances of a Japanese democracy. If those who wish to go back to it were to face the past honestly, they would know this, which is precisely why they persist in their refusal to do so.

THREE

ENLIGHTENMENT VALUES

I NEVER DARED TO BE RADICAL WHEN
YOUNG, FOR FEAR IT WOULD MAKE
ME CONSERVATIVE WHEN OLD.

—*Robert Frost*

Tocqueville took a view of Islam and democracy that is still the conventional one. Muhammed, he wrote, "brought down from heaven and put into the Koran not religious doctrines only, but political maxims, criminal and civil laws, and scientific theories. The Gospels, on the other hand, deal only with the general relations between man and God and man and man. Beyond that, they teach nothing and do not oblige people to believe anything. That alone, among a thousand reasons, is enough to show that Islam will not be able to hold its power long in ages of enlightenment and democracy, while Christianity is destined to reign in such ages, as in all others."[1]

The great French Catholic thinker was not an expert on Islam. And comparing the Koran with the Gospels alone is not quite sufficient. Tocqueville conveniently forgot to mention that the Old Testament (let alone the Talmud) contains politics and laws too. Moreover, as Tocqueville himself observed in the United States, the most irrational, and indeed unenlightened, beliefs can easily hold sway over the citizens of democracies. And the citizens he saw were not Muslims. The question is whether people who hold such beliefs can still agree to play by the rules of democratic government. By and large, American Christians could, and still can. Is there reason to believe that Muslims cannot?

Thinkers of the Enlightenment were divided on this issue. But some radical Spinozists, such as Pierre Bayle, took the view that Islam was superior to Judaism and Christianity because it was more tolerant and less superstitious. Eighteenth-century philosophes also remembered that it was scholars from the Muslim world—though not always Muslims themselves; some were Jews—who had been responsible for passing on the classics of Greek philosophy in Arabic translation. Like Confucius, the twelfth-century philosopher Ibn Rushd (Averroes) was even compared to Spinoza as a paragon of reason.[2]

Democracy is, in any case, neither new nor strange to many Muslims. The Indian population includes around 150 million Muslims. Like most democracies, the Indian system of government is far from perfect, but its flaws—corruption, demagoguery, crime, caste-based fury, and so on—have nothing to do with the contents of the Koran. Turkish democracy is equally imperfect, but the ideological "secularists" are as much to blame for its defects as the Islamists, possibly more so. And Indonesia, the largest Muslim majority nation in the world, is now one of the few functioning democracies in Southeast Asia.

Still, it is certainly the case that Middle Eastern, predominantly Muslim countries have tended to be autocratic. There are many possible reasons—cultural, historical, political—but it should be remembered that except for Iran, and briefly Afghanistan, Middle Eastern dictatorships are secular. Nasserism borrowed heavily from Marxism. Saddam Hussein was an Arab fascist. Egyptian and Syrian strongmen crushed Islamist movements, such as the Muslim Brotherhood, as ruthlessly as any nineteenth-century European colonial regime might have done. The main target of radical religious activism has been the corrupt secular police state. Because the corruption of autocratic Middle Eastern elites is associated with the decadent, unbelieving West (not entirely unjustly, since the West continues, perhaps faute de mieux, to support these elites), Europe and the United States have become prime targets for the religious radicals. This in turn has inflamed the passions of young Muslims in Europe, who have found a ready-made cause to kill and die for.

However, the fear of Islam among Europeans is not limited to concern about revolutionary Islamist violence. The worry is more what Tocqueville articulated: that Islam is incompatible with what we now call "Enlightenment values," or "Western values" (as though these were identical), and that the presence of a large Muslim minority in the West will damage, if not destroy, values that we have come to take for granted (forgetting how recently they were acquired), such as free speech and equal rights for women and homosexuals. Since it is assumed, in time-honored fashion when it comes to unpopular minorities, that Muslims will consistently produce more children than non-Muslims, there is a fear of being "swamped," of losing the European identity, of seeing the continent turned into "Eurabia." Many Europeans are not just frightened of religious violence; they are anxious about being "Islamized."

Alarm about minorities cut off from the rest of society is widespread—alarm, that is, when it comes to Muslims; Chinatowns and Hassidic communities are treated with indifference. The latter are peaceful and too small to worry about. The worry concerns what philosophers and political thinkers have been agonizing about for centuries, at least as far back as the time of Confucius: how to constitute a political community on the basis of common ethics, mores, beliefs, or laws. In present-day terms, if citizens fail to share common values, how can democracy survive?

Even if one believes, as I do, that shared values are not essential for a democracy to function, as long as citizens abide by the laws, the worry is legitimate when a significant number of people are prepared to break those laws for ideological reasons. Since some of the most ferocious enemies of liberal democracy now happen to be revolutionary Islamists, the concern about Muslims who express views that are hostile to Western society is understandable and must be faced. The problem is all the more acute, since the violent revolutionaries are no longer strangers from faraway countries but young people born and bred in Europe whose first languages are not Arabic but English, French, or Dutch.

A cursory look at some of the people responsible for atrocities should dispel one commonly held idea, introduced by Bernard Lewis and popularized by Samuel Huntington, that we are dealing with a "clash of civilizations." The men who came to western European countries in the 1960s from Turkey and North Africa to work in factories or clean the streets were indeed from a different world. Often illiterate, usually from rural areas, the first generation of *Gastarbeiter* had customs and traditions that were strange to most Europeans and might have become a source of conflict. In fact, content to make enough money to send home to their families and too overworked to engage in any political action, these men were no threat to anyone.

When the foreign workers failed to go home, contrary to expectation, some European governments allowed them to bring over their families. The arrival of large numbers of migrants in old working-class areas inevitably caused tensions with the locals. But complaints were usually dismissed by lazy bureaucrats, anxious politicians, or ideological social workers as marks of European racism. It was easier to ignore the problems and cloak passivity in anti-racist, anti-colonialist, multiculturalist rhetoric.

That the habits of new immigrants often clashed with prevailing norms of mainstream society, however, hardly constituted a threat to the continued existence of liberal democracy, let alone Western civilization. The real threat comes from a radical fundamentalist ideology, especially in the violent form of holy war. But the new wave of fundamentalism—a trend that is far from unique to Islam—is not the expression of a traditional culture or civilization but a modern, global phenomenon. The same goes for the revolutionary holy war. As Olivier Roy, the most astute European scholar of modern Islam, explains: "[Neofundamentalism] thrives on the loss of cultural identity: the young radicals are indeed perfectly 'Westernized'. Among the born-again and the converts (numerous young women who want to wear the veil belong to these categories), Islam is seen not as a cultural relic but as a religion that is universal and global and reaches beyond specific cultures, just like evangelicalism or Pentecostalism."[3]

Mohammed Bouyeri, the murderer of the Dutch filmmaker Theo van Gogh, was born and raised in Amsterdam. His father came from Morocco in the 1960s. Mohammed was not interested in religion when he grew up. His knowledge of Islam was rudimentary. He preferred to get high and chase girls. Like many young people, he was sensitive to slights and rejections. As a member of a widely despised minority, he was perhaps more than usually sensitive. Alienated from the village culture of his parents, ill at ease in the country of his birth, he was ripe for the seduction of a new identity promising purity, moral superiority, and power. Radical Islamism came to him first from a roaming preacher exiled from Syria, and then from the Internet. Much of what Mohammed knows about his faith, a purist, brutal version of Islam, he downloaded from various Web sites, mostly in English, catering to the disaffected and resentful in search of a common cause. If he had been a Russian in the early twentieth century, he might have been an anarchist. If he had been German in the 1970s, he could easily have joined the Red Army Faction. Since he was a

"Moroccan" in twenty-first-century Holland, he was born again as a holy warrior for an Islamic utopia.

The story of Mohammad Sidique Khan, ringleader of the 7/7 bomb attack in the London underground, offers an even better illustration of Olivier Roy's account. Born in Leeds in 1974, he grew up in Beeston, a rundown suburb with a large immigrant population, many of whom came from the same tribal area of Pakistan. Drug addiction was ravaging an already isolated and impoverished community. When a number of young men, including Khan, formed a group called the Mullah Boys to combat crime and drug addiction, older people welcomed the initiative, even if some of them were alarmed by the type of militant Islam adopted by the group.

Khan, known as "Sid" to his classmates, was not a natural hater. He had white friends and, like his Dutch namesake, Mohammed Bouyeri, was full of ideas on how to better the lot of his community. After finishing school, he studied for a business degree at Leeds Metropolitan University, where he met his future wife, a Muslim of Indian origin. He married her ("out of tribe," as it were) against the wishes of his parents. Again like Bouyeri, he was an active mentor of troubled youths, hence his interest in the Mullah Boys. It was through them that he became interested in Wahhabism, the sectarian, fundamentalist faith sponsored by Saudi Arabia.

The great attraction of Wahhabism for dislocated people everywhere is its purism, its lack of roots in any particular culture or tradition. The Urdu-speaking preachers of his parents' generation didn't appeal to Khan because he barely spoke Urdu, and because, as a Yorkshire lad, he had only a shallow connection with the tribal culture they came from. Wahhabism is promoted, on the Internet and elsewhere, in English. It holds out the promise of a purely Islamic state. In its most militant form, this brand of political Islam has a revolutionary ideology that appeals for social or political reasons perhaps more than theological ones. In the words of Hassan Butt, a former recruiter in Britain for holy warriors: "Here come the Islamists and they give you an identity ... you don't need Pakistan or Britain. You can be anywhere in the world and this identity will stick with you and give you a sense of belonging."[4]

Khan not only found religion, he found a revolutionary cause. Marrying a woman outside his Barelvi tribe was an act of defiance on Khan's part. But so was his extreme Islamism. His family actually tried to steer him away from his radical path by appealing to their own cultural tradition. A traditional religious man, a *pir*, was asked to talk sense to him. It didn't work. By the time Khan committed murder and suicide with two other boys from Beeston by planting bombs on the subway train, he had severed all his family ties. As Butt explains: "When you're cut off from your family, the jihadi network then becomes your family. It becomes your backbone and support."[5]

Conrad described the type beautifully in novels such as *The Secret Agent* and *Under Western Eyes*: the angry young man buried in the anonymous masses of our great cities, waiting to blow himself and others up in a final act that will wipe out his confusion; violent death as the balm to a wounded sense of personal inadequacy. An act of revenge against the indifference of the outside world. In the cases of Mohammed Bouyeri and Mohammad Sidique Khan, they justified their acts by embracing a peculiar and above all modern vision of Islam.

•   •   •

Since the holy warriors in Europe are linked, however tenuously, to a world wide web of revolutionary Islamist fury, they must be taken seriously as a security threat. Their networks should be monitored, infiltrated, and crushed.

Apart from the global scale, and the lethal possibilities of modern technology, there is little new about this. The use of terror, as propaganda or as a tactic of violent fantasists, has always been there. The fact, however, that in this case it is inspired by revolutionary Islam complicates matters. It has led many people to conflate the threat of political extremism with customs and traditions associated with the religion that do not conform to the conventions of modern liberalism: Islam as a threat to the Enlightened West, as the Trojan horse that will "Islamize" Europe.

Discussion of the Enlightenment in newspaper columns, political speeches, and so forth is something new. Until the perception took hold that the West was under siege, the Enlightenment was an academic subject. It is no longer. Historically, the Enlightenment consisted of many things: the anti-clericalism of Spinoza's early Enlightenment, the rationalism of the French philosophes, the pragmatism of the Scottish and English Enlightenment. Some philosophers were religious, some actively anti-religious. If Voltaire, Diderot, and Locke were men of the Enlightenment, then so was the Marquis de Sade, who took the destruction of Christian morality to its logical conclusion. If there is no God to prescribe for us the difference between good and evil, then why should the free-spirited individual not act on his desires, no matter how violent or perverted? Anything short of that would be hypocritical, and besides, nothing, no matter how depraved, in individual human behavior can ever be as wicked as the cruelty inflicted by political regimes claiming to be blessed by God.

Sade is not whom most modern defenders of Enlightenment values have in mind. I suspect that some of the same people who now wish to defend the Enlightened West against the threat of Islam would, a century ago, have spoken of Christendom. There are traces of this even among commentators who used to rank themselves among the

Left. Melanie Phillips, for example, has become one of the clearest voices in Britain advocating vigilance against Islam. Her widely read book *Londonistan* is a chronicle of the ways in which Muslim organizations in Britain, aided and abetted by non-Muslim "appeasers," have undermined the national identity. What is this national identity? Phillips: "At the heart of this unpicking of national identity lies a repudiation of Christianity, the founding faith of the nation and the fundamental source of its values, including its sturdy individualism and profound love of liberty."[6] And the strategy of Al-Qaeda?: "Dethrone Christianity, and the job of subjugating the West is halfway done."[7]

This view is not shared by all European defenders of Enlightenment values, some of whom believe that these include anti-religious or atheist values. In France, the Muslims are actually paying the price for the long domination of the Catholic Church. Voltaire's *écrasez l'infame*—"wipe out the dangerous nonsense!"—was aimed at the authority of Catholic priests. It is now invoked against women who wear headscarves in public schools. It was, in any case, certainly not meant as a defense of Christendom.

A key element of Enlightenment thinking in the eighteenth century was the claim to universal validity. Human reason is not bound by culture, creed, or tradition; it is universal. And so are the fruits of reason, such as scientific inquiry, criticism, and the right to exercise these faculties freely, without political or religious interference. Viewing one's own culture and society with a critical eye was part of Enlightenment thinking, as was the exploration of, and translation from, other cultures and civilizations. Orientalist scholarship came from the Enlightenment spirit, as did Schlegel's translations of Shakespeare's plays. It was precisely the universalist claim that made the Enlightenment suspect to many "progressives" in the 1960s and 1970s, who saw it as a neo-colonialist imposition of

"Western values" on former colonial subjects in the Third World. One of the many ironies playing through the current debates in Europe is that these same values are now defended ferociously against Islam by the very same former progressives.[8]

Enlightenment values are often interpreted as Western values, not only by their erstwhile critics but by their current defenders. The main enemy is not just Islam, or Islamism, but the Western appeasers, who have undermined the West by their promotion of moral relativism and multiculturalism.

Like any idea, when it becomes dogma, multiculturalism is often misguided. A dogmatic moral relativist refuses to criticize the moral values of other cultures, especially non-Western cultures, because they are all equally valid in their own time and place. Anyone who disagrees with this view is swiftly denounced as a racist. Multiculturalism, as an ideology, is based on the same idea. Immigrants must be encouraged to stick to the traditions of their ancestors, which are not only as valid as those of the West but in fact usually superior. At best this is deeply condescending. Melanie Phillips mentions the case of education authorities in London trying to prevent ethnic minority children from watching the Queen Mother's funeral on television because "it wouldn't mean anything to them."[9]

Multiculturalism has been particularly strong in former imperial powers, where the postcolonial intelligentsia were prone to feelings of guilt when dealing with the non-Western world. Anti-imperialism and anti-racism survived as the main currents of the postwar European Left, even as the appeal of Marxist ideology slowly faded. Gilles Kepel, the French author of many books on Islam, has argued that British and Dutch multiculturalism echo old colonial practices of indirect rule through organized religious and ethnic communities. One could argue with equal justice that colonial rule echoed the multireligious and multi-ethnic nature of Britain and the Netherlands. At any rate, this "communal" approach, he says, prevents successful integration of Muslims and other immigrants in Europe because they are treated as distinct cultural groups. France, where every citizen is theoretically treated equally as an individual and communal identities are not officially recognized, does not appear to have this problem.

In fact, as the periodic bursts of serious violence in immigrant areas of large French cities show, France does have a problem. Insisting that collective identities should play no role in the public sphere hides the problems of minorities but does not solve them, and possibly makes them worse. Colonial guilt sticks to the French just as much as to the Dutch or British. But the pretense that collective identities, with their own histories and sensitivities, don't count serves as a kind of camouflage, a bit like the claim of former East Germans that since they were all "anti-fascists" they were untainted by the Nazi past. And the Nazi past, no less than memories of colonial conquest, still haunts European debates about culture and race.

Anti-racism, as an attitude, stems not only from colonial guilt but also from the ghastly fate of the European Jews under German occupation. As a rhetorical device, the Third Reich is often invoked against those suspected of racism. People who complain about the social habits of immigrant neighbors (loud calls to prayer, unaccustomed food smells, and so forth) or about rising crime in immigrant areas are told that such xenophobic, or "Islamophobic," attitudes lead straight to the gas chambers.

But memories of the war can also be turned in the opposite direction. Efforts to accommodate Muslims, to find common ground, to tolerate views that do not necessarily conform to modern liberal values, are akin to Chamberlain's appeasement of Hitler—or worse, comparable to collaboration with the Nazis. To those who fear the "Islamization" of Europe, it is forever 1938. One alarmist author, an American living in Europe, wrote ominously about Europe's "Weimar Moment."[10] Melanie Phillips was compared in a New York newspaper to "the few who spoke out in Britain against appeasing Hitler in the 1930s."[11] The West is at war not only with Islamist revolutionaries but with "Islamo-fascism." As Olivier Roy observed about the rather too glib use of Munich 1938, "many who take themselves for Churchill write like Celine, without his style."[12]

Phillips believes, like Tocqueville, and indeed like the Muslims she opposes, that moral values collapse without religion: "secular humanism had opened Pandora's Box."[13] But Christianity, or Judeo-Christianity, is not the only way to define the West.

The most interesting politician to have tapped the popular fear of Islam is the late Dutch populist Pim Fortuyn. Like right-wing demagogues in France, Austria, and other parts of Europe, Fortuyn exploited a sense shared by many people, not just in Europe, of losing their moorings in a global network of multinational corporations and supranational bureaucracies. In some ways, such anxieties mirror those of the young children of immigrants who look for reassurance and a new identity in pure visions of Islam. Fortuyn and other populists led a rebellion against the political and intellectual elites who are blamed for everything that provokes these anxieties: immigration, the European Union, the shifting global currents of money and services.

What Fortuyn offered was a way back to a cozier, more familiar, more homogeneous land, where the natives were still among themselves, so to speak, undisturbed by odd food smells, strange calls to prayer, unruly street kids with foreign accents, Eurocrats in Brussels, and all the confusions associated with "globalization." It was a fantasy, of course, of a society that never really existed. And even if it did, there would be no way back.

But Fortuyn had another, more original, and altogether more modern reason to stoke the fear of Muslims in Dutch society. Unusually for a politician running on an anti-immigration platform, Fortuyn was a public figure who flaunted his homosexuality. Asked why he disliked Muslims, he replied: "What do you mean, dislike Muslims? I go to bed with them." Like many people who joined the struggle against "Islamo-fascism," Fortuyn was once a leftist. He also grew up in a strict Roman Catholic family and retained a fondness for the rituals and ceremonies of his church. But the West that he sought to defend against Islam did not conform to the Vatican's notion of civilization. Nor was it in every respect like his cozy vision of Holland in the 1950s, when families spent their Sundays listening to Christian sermons on the radio. Fortuyn's notion of the West had a distinct post-1960s flavor: equal rights for women and gays, sexual freedom, and so on. That's why he said: "I don't feel like having to go through the emancipation of women and homosexuals all over again."[14]

•　　　•　　　•

The event that pushed many former multiculturalists, anti-racists, and pro–Third Worldists to join conservatives in their stand against Islam was the burning of Salman Rushdie's novel *The Satanic Verses*. Rushdie, born in India, the son of wealthy parents, and educated at Rugby School and King's College, Cambridge, was himself a prominent figure in the leftist metropolitan intelligentsia, a postcolonial literary hero, happy to denounce Western imperialism in all its forms. His was the cosmopolitan voice of London and Bombay. A non-believer from a well-to-do Muslim family, with a fondness for pagan libertinism, Rushdie is an example of the cultural mélange that has enriched the artistic life of postwar Europe. Instead of reaching for a purist religious identity, Rushdie embraced the freedom to pick and choose from the various cultures at hand. His novel is not so much an attack on Islam as it is on the fanatical fetish of ethnic, cultural, or religious purity. His playful, irreverent treatment of religious texts—verses dictated to the Prophet by Satan—was a worse insult to fanatics than an all-out attack on their faith.

It wasn't just religious fanatics who were burning his book, however—often, most probably, without having read a word of it—but the less privileged sons and grandsons of the British Empire, born and raised in bleak concrete suburbs of broken-down industrial cities in provincial England. This came as a great shock to the left-wing intelligentsia. Rushdie was not only "one of us," but he had been on *their* side, the side of the poor and oppressed people of the postcolonial world. And here were these coarse provincial youths, their minds inflamed by primitive imams, burning a literary novel and conjuring up images in the minds of horrified liberal intellectuals of storm troopers torching "degenerate" masterpieces in 1933.

The Rushdie case split the Left, but also the Right, and indeed the Muslims too. Some conservatives, especially religious conservatives, sympathized with the passions of Muslims who felt insulted by what they regarded as Rushdie's blasphemy. Britain's blasphemy laws cover only the Anglican faith. When spokesmen for the Islamic Foundation, established in Leicester in 1973 with Saudi funding, demanded an amendment to cover the Muslim faith as well, they received some support from pious Christians, though not from the Anglican archbishop, who was in favor of scrapping the blasphemy law altogether. The historian Hugh Trevor-Roper, not a religious man at all, declared that he would not "shed a tear, if some British Muslims, deploring Mr. Rushdie's manners, were to waylay him in a dark street and seek to improve them."[15] Other conservatives were as appalled by the attacks on Rushdie as were his liberal friends.

The Islamic Foundation formed part of the UK Islamic Mission, whose stated aim was to "establish Islamic social order in the United Kingdom." The Saudi money and the stated aim are not reassuring. But the Islamic Foundation still sought to promote its cause by democratic means as a pressure group. The Rushdie case gave the Islamic Foundation an opportunity to play a national role, as though it were representing all Muslims. Burning books and violent demonstrations were not their thing, however. This was done by the kind of "tribal Muslims" (the community from which Mohammad Sidique Khan, the 7/7 bomber, sprang) whom the more sophisticated Islamists of the UK Islamic Mission despised. The book-burners were represented by the Bradford Council of Mosques. And they only got going after Muslims in India staged demonstrations for their own reasons (the book was banned first in India). But the most famous exploiter of the case was Iran's Ayatollah Khomeini, who aspired to be the leader of all Muslims in the world and issued his deadly fatwa against the British author, as though he were an Islamic pope. In the end, Muslims proved to be much too diverse, in and outside Britain, to be unified. The attempt, in Britain, by the late Dr. Kalim Siddiqui, a Pakistani immigrant who started his career as a journalist for the liberal *Guardian* newspaper, to rally all the protesters against Rushdie's book and set up a Muslim parliament, ended in failure.[16]

Some politicians and intellectuals of the Left remained wedded to their old Third Worldist instincts out of opportunism or conviction. The British Labour Party MP Keith Vaz led a demonstration in Leicester carrying a banner showing Rushdie's head, sprouting devil's horns, superimposed on a dog. To the knee-jerk defenders of any non-Western cause, Rushdie had no right to offend the Muslims. Many others, however, rallied round the cause of free speech and began their break away from long-held convictions about the role of the West and the privileged place for different cultures inside its borders.

This was not just understandable; defending an author's freedom of expression was right. But the way in which old positions were abandoned sometimes showed the typical zeal of conversion, a zeal compounded by a sour sense of betrayal. The German sociologist Jürgen Habermas has described the current climate in Europe as a *Kulturkampf* between secularists and multiculturalists. This German term for a European culture war was first coined in the 1870s when Bismarck, the Iron Chancellor, unleashed his political assault on the German Catholics, who were wrongly suspected of being instruments of the Vatican under Pope Pius IX, whose reactionary ideas on papal infallibility were regarded as a threat to the secular German Reich. Jesuits were expelled, Catholic orders disbanded, and religious institutions taken over by the state.

Many contemporary secularists once rebelled against everything they saw as reactionary in Western life: the church of course, but also sexual mores, racial prejudices, capitalism, gender inequalities, and so on. They stood up, in theory at least, for the poor and oppressed, victims of racism at home and imperialism abroad. No matter how oppressive the leaders of the oppressed, they stood by them in solidarity against the vastly more oppressive system, as they saw it, of neo-colonialist Western capitalism.

Most of those who called for the head of Salman Rushdie had family roots in the Third World. But in many cases, Islam was not their main inspiration. Indeed, many of the angry young men were not religious at all. And the conversion of those who were often came late. Kenan Malik, a British journalist and academic, visited the Bradford Council of Mosques in 1989, a few weeks after the burning of Rushdie's book. There he ran into Hassan, an old friend and comrade in the Socialist Workers Party, of which both had once been members. Malik and Hassan used to believe in a radical socialist solution for ethnic and economic inequality. Theirs was a secular, universalist, political ideal, a radical echo of Enlightenment philosophy. When this ideal failed to materialize, disillusion beset the socialist, antiracist ranks. And among children of immigrants, a kind of tribal retrenchment took place, replacing the universal ideal. This tendency was encouraged by a Left which, more and more, abandoned Marxism in favor of identity politics. Anti-racism was no longer interpreted in terms of class warfare but as a claim to separate identities, a protest against cultural oppression.

When Malik asked his friend what on earth he was doing at the Bradford Council of Mosques, Hassan replied that he was involved in the campaign "to silence the blasphemer." Malik could no longer recognize his old comrade, whom he remembered as a good-time type who used to enjoy chasing girls, drinking, and watching the Arsenal football club. "No need to look so shocked," said Hassan. "I've had it with the white Left. I'd lost my sense of who I am and where I came from. So I came back to Bradford to rediscover it. We need to defend our dignity as Muslims, to defend our values and beliefs, and not allow anyone—racist or Rushdie—to trample over them."[17] Malik followed the other path, of leftists who joined the *Kulturkampf* against multiculturalism.

What Hassan's story illustrates is that the pull of religious ideology is not usually a theological one but has everything to do with political rage. To explain the Rushdie case in terms of the Koran, or the Muslim tradition, is misleading. The turn to religion to forge a sense of self, of community, of strength is akin to what happened in the United States in the 1960s, when a political movement in which black and white activists had stood together did not produce the desired results. Martin Luther King was assassinated. Malcolm X was assassinated. Black Power, and The Nation of Islam, asserting black identity, and rejecting white society, became the new politics. This was the kind of choice made by Hassan but also by Mohammad Sidique Khan. The killings on the London underground began with the burning of Rushdie's book. Both acts were perpetrated in the name of Islam, not the traditional Islam of rural Pakistan but a new purist, reinvention of Islam. Politics and faith had converged in a fatal mix.

Black Power was regarded by many white liberals as a betrayal. Was this their reward for having braved the police dogs and guns of Birmingham and Selma together with the Negroes? In his famous essay, "My Negro Problem—and Ours,"[18] the New York intellectual Norman Podhoretz described his bitter experiences with blacks in his native Brooklyn in the 1940s. Coming from a socialist Jewish family, he was always taught to see the Negro as weak and underprivileged, a figure to be protected against injustice and discrimination. In fact, the Negroes he knew in Brooklyn were not weak at all but tough enough to beat him up in the schoolyard. He envied their toughness and began to despise "the writers and intellectuals and artists who romanticize the Negroes, and pander to them," and "all the white liberals who permit the Negroes to blackmail them into adopting a double standard of moral judgment."[19]

Former leftists, like Podhoretz, who turned into neoconservatives in the 1960s felt betrayed by Negroes who refused to be grateful for white solidarity; and they felt betrayed by white liberals who "pandered" to the Negroes, criticized the Vietnam War, and attacked Israel. They, too, like Hassan, though for different reasons, had had it with the white Left.

When twelve young Muslims in Bradford stood trial in 1982 for having made petrol bombs to defend themselves against white racist gangs, most liberals supported them. In the event "the Bradford 12" were acquitted. When Bradford Muslims burned Rushdie's book just seven years later, the sense of betrayal was keen.

The British playwright David Edgar described the feelings of former leftists, who once joined far Left organizations to support the poor and the oppressed. When their causes collapsed in violence and corruption, rage was turned not just against the parties but against the poor themselves: "The discovery that the poor do not necessarily respond to their victimhood with uncomplaining resignation is as traumatic as the complementary perception that they don't always behave in a spirit of selfless heroism." It is hard enough, he continues, "to be fooled by the party; even harder to accept that you deluded yourself into believing that the poor are, by virtue of their poverty, uniquely saintly or strong. No surprise that this realisation turns into a sense of personal betrayal, which turns outwards into blame."[20]

This explains the harsh tone of the present *Kulturkampf*—this and the constantly revived memories of fascism and a shrill dogmatic attitude that remains from old leftist positions. David Edgar, himself an old campaigner of the Left, put it well: "As former victims of political delusion, these defectors claim a unique authority. But there is something quite particular about spending the second half of your life taking revenge on the first. Inevitably, however complete the conversion, what defectors think and do now is coloured by what they thought and did before."[21]

The debate over Islam in Europe is held less in a spirit of finding the truth through open disagreement than of separating friends from foes and fingering traitors, appeasers, and collaborators. This mimics the worst years of the cold war and deliberately echoes the rhetoric of World War II. Islamist radicalism is worrying enough. But we have to recognize it for what it is. To confuse Islamism (let alone Islam per se) with Hitler's Nazis or Stalin's Soviet Empire is not the best way to come to grips with it.

•   •   •

The second iconic figure in the European debate on Islam, after Salman Rushdie, is the activist Ayaan Hirsi Ali. Her story, which began in her native Somalia and is continuing in Europe and the United States, is, like so many others, one of disillusion and conversion. Growing up in exile in Kenya (her father was an opponent of the Somali dictator Mohammed Siad Barre), she became a Muslim fundamentalist in a fit of teenage rebellion. She covered her body in a *hijab*, was sympathetic to the Ayatollah's regime in Iran, and when she heard of Rushdie's "blasphemy" she wished him dead.

Hirsi Ali changed after being forced to marry a distant relative in Canada. Although a democrat in politics, her father was a conservative in family matters. En route to Canada, she decided to bolt across the Dutch border, where she applied for political asylum, claiming that she was fleeing the Somalian civil war. Still religious, though no longer in a radical way, she learned Dutch, worked to help fellow refugees, studied political science at Leyden University, and read the *Atheist Manifesto*, written by a Dutch professor of philosophy. Western life, for her, came as a liberation. Bit by bit, religious constraints fell away.

She lived with a Dutch boyfriend, drank alcohol, and gradually became a convinced atheist.

Since Hirsi Ali was concerned with the lot of immigrant women, oppressed by their husbands and fathers in the name of tradition or Islam, the liberal-Left Dutch Labor Party seemed to be her natural home. She did some research for the party's think tank. But her conclusions could not have been less congenial to the multicultural party line. Islamic schools should be closed, she argued, immigration limited, and state subsidy for religious education, guaranteed by Article 23 of the Dutch constitutions, stopped. Leftists are in fact not the main supporters of Article 23; the Christian parties are. Nonetheless, her views on Islam and immigration were not considered helpful, especially when she called the Prophet "a pervert" and a "tyrant." Several Muslims tried to take her to court, without success, for insulting people on the grounds of their faith.

If Hassan, in Bradford, was fed up with the white Left, so was Hirsi Ali. But she turned not to radical Islam but to the conservative Liberal Party, whose leaders had been warning for some time against the dangers of Islam to the Western way of life. She became more and more outspoken on talk shows and TV programs, and was offered a seat in the Dutch parliament partly as a way to get government protection against Islamist extremists who were threatening to kill her. She spoke out against "honor killings" of women, a cause she described as her "holy mission."[22] She wrote the script for a short film, titled *Submission*, in which Koranic texts about female oppression were projected onto the naked bodies of veiled women. Theo van Gogh directed the film and was murdered soon after it was shown on television. Calling himself the "village idiot," he had refused to seek protection and as a private citizen was not offered any.

That violent Islamism is dangerous is not really in dispute. The question is whether the main cause of this violence is theological or political. Hirsi Ali takes the former view. As a convert to atheism, she finds little favor with any religion, but has a special bone to pick with Islam. The justification for 9/11, she wrote, was "the core of Islam," and the "inhuman act of those nineteen hijackers" its "logical outcome."[23] Islam, therefore, must be reformed and the Koran reinterpreted—and even, where necessary, edited or censured. Only then can the threat of radical Islamism be countered.

There is something to be said for this position. Whether she, as an atheist, is best placed to be a religious reformer is another matter. But there is little room for nuance in the *Kulturkampf* of contemporary Europe. Ayaan Hirsi Ali became a polarizing figure in the Netherlands: you were either for her or against her. Denunciations flew both ways. Those who promoted her cause were accused of being right-wing Islamophobes, seduced by her dark female beauty. Critics were called, at best, patronizing (because she is a woman) or naïve—the "useful idiots" of our time—but more commonly condemned as appeasers, traitors, or enemies of Enlightenment values.

Ayaan Hirsi Ali had plans to move to the United States even before events in her adopted country made her into an international cause célèbre. First, she was given notice to leave her secured apartment in The Hague after neighbors, anxious about security risks and declining property values, had successfully taken the government to court. Then, Hirsi Ali's friend and ally in the conservative Liberal Party, the hard-line minister of immigration Rita Verdonk, decided, while running for the party leadership, to get tough on refugees who had applied for asylum under false pretenses. When Hirsi Ali told an interviewer that she, too, had lied, Verdonk threatened to revoke her citizenship, a threat that was swiftly withdrawn after a furious all-night debate in parliament, which left Verdonk a diminished figure.

By the time Hirsi Ali had moved to the United States to join the American Enterprise Institute in Washington, D.C., the *Kulturkampf* had gone global. A petition was drawn up, and was signed by such prominent critics of political Islam as the Canadian activist Irshad Manji, stating that the Dutch treatment of Hirsi Ali exposed "the political agenda of the Dutch government which is to threaten and silence all opponents of Political Islam and defenders of secularism."[24]

Buried under all the posturing, petition writing, and misinformation was a reasoned debate on the merits of Hirsi Ali's arguments. Instead, Americans wrote smug articles about European cowardice and the superiority of the land of the free (where visas were becoming increasingly difficult to come by for people unfortunate enough to be born in Muslim countries or to just have a Muslim name). When the Dutch government decided, without much tact or grace, that it would no longer pay for Hirsi Ali's security when she became a permanent resident of the United States, a new round of denunciations and breast-beating ensued. Not that the Dutch policy was any different from Britain's or France's, let alone that of the United States, which does not even pay for the security of its own private citizens at home. But "Ayaan" had become so much more than a person; she was a symbol around whom the adversaries in the *Kulturkampf* clashed.

This time it was the French who boasted of their superior custodianship of liberty. President Sarkozy stated that France would protect oppressed women all over the world, including Ayaan Hirsi Ali. Bernard-Henri Lévy, the celebrity philosopher, made speeches about "Ayaan" being "disowned" by her "spiritual homeland." The very "soul of

Europe" was at stake, and France should grant her citizen-ship forthwith. Hirsi Ali was duly grateful: "It's the outrage, expressed by French intellectuals at the decision of the current Dutch administration to stop protecting me, that gives me strength and hope. Strength, to go on fighting in-justices to women in the name of Islam. And hope that my life will be protected, if not by the Dutch government, then hopefully by the French government.... Je serais honorée d'avoir la possibilité de devenir française. Merci beaucoup. [I would consider it an honour to become a French citizen. Thank you very much.]"[25]

In the event, France did not follow up on its offer to pay for her protection, and Hirsi Ali remains a Dutch citizen, living in the United States. And in October 2007, Salman Rushdie himself piled on yet one more layer of hyperbole, once again deliberately invoking memories of another, very different time. Ayaan Hirsi Ali, he wrote in the *Los Angeles Times*, "may be the first refugee from Western Europe since the Holocaust."[26]

•   •   •

"The words 'tolerance' and 'respect' have lost their in-nocence."[27] So a major Dutch daily newspaper informed its readers after Queen Beatrix had pleaded for "diver-sity" and "tolerance" in her Christmas speech in 2007. Geert Wilders, a right-wing politician with a fierce anti-Muslim agenda, went further: the Queen's speech made him "vomit." It was full of "multi-cultural rubbish."[28]

Tolerance was once considered one of the greatest fruits of the Enlightenment.[29] John Locke, whose idea of toler-ance was not boundless, had this to say: "The toleration of those that differ from others in matters of religion is so agreeable to the Gospel of Jesus Christ, and to the genuine reason of mankind, that it seems monstrous for men to be so blind as not to perceive the necessity and advantage of it in so clear a light."[30]

Locke believed that political authority should not be extended to matters of religion. Although he clearly favored Protestant Christianity, he left space for other faiths. The limits of Locke's tolerance concerned those who did not believe in any God at all, a position still held by some religious believers today.

However, Locke was far from condemning tolerance as a form of weakness. Yet that is now a popular view with faint echoes of past anti-liberal positions: tolerance as a typical sign of liberal decadence, as a form of "moral relativism," nihilism, indifference, even contempt, because, in the words of the French writer Pascal Bruckner, "it assumes that certain communities are incapable of modernising."[31] To be tolerant of the views and customs of religious minorities that go against the mainstream of modern opinion (on sexuality, the role of women, and so forth) is an example of tolerating intolerance, of letting people stew in their own juice without caring about their well-being, or indeed the well-being of Western liberal democracy. The Dutch novelist Leon de Winter, in a critical review of my book about the murder of Theo van Gogh,[32] quoted Karl Popper's words from *The Open Society and Its Enemies* (1945): "Unlimited tolerance must lead to the disappearance of tolerance. If we extend unlimited tolerance even to those who are intolerant, if we are not prepared to defend a tolerant society against the onslaught of the intolerant, then the tolerant will be destroyed, and tolerance with them."[33]

Popper was right, if by "onslaught" he meant more than intolerant opinions. He was a little vague on this point. Suppressing "intolerant philosophies," he argued, would "certainly be most unwise" as long as "we can counter them by rational argument and keep them in check by public opinion." But defenders of the open society, he said, should "claim, in the name of tolerance, the right not to tolerate the intolerant" if people were "not prepared to meet us on the level of rational argument." For such people might well end up teaching their followers "to answer arguments by the use of their fists or pistols."[34]

The question is when suppression should commence: before or after the use of fists and pistols? Most Western democracies have laws against inciting hatred or violence. Interpreting such incitements is not always easy, and the laws are often too vague. The books of more than one religion contain violent passages. These can be used as incitements, but that is not always the intention (or Jews celebrating Passover would be guilty of extraordinarily threatening language). Social intolerance, in the sense of excluding or even despising non-believers, or homosexuals, or adulterous women, or whatnot, is not in itself an invitation to use violence. A democracy, in order to preserve free speech, should err on the side of caution in these matters and suppress opinions only when a direct link to violent behavior can be proven.

There is something else, however, underlying the calls to stop being so tolerant. It is an old indictment against liberalism—the idea that the liberal state stands for nothing, is, by dint of its neutrality in questions of belief, quite literally unbelieving. When Pascal Bruckner advocates the duty to "modernize" people, he speaks as a radical French republican with a strong conviction that the state must shape the thoughts and behavior of individual citizens. In its most dogmatic form this resulted in the Terror of 1793, with the slogan: "No freedom for the enemies of freedom." That President George W. Bush, who was neither a noted Francophile nor, one would have thought, a keen defender of the French Revolution, almost revived this phrase is one of the bitter ironies thrown up by his term in office.

Those who believe that the state has a duty to instill cultural, moral, or religious beliefs are convinced that we are doomed to decadence if it fails to do so. In the true spirit of *Kulturkampf*, Melanie Phillips cries out that "Britain is currently locked in such a spiral of decadence, self-loathing and sentimentality, that it is incapable of seeing that it is setting itself up for cultural immolation."[35] She, of course, wishes to restore Christianity as the nation's cultural spine. Bruckner and other believers in the Jacobin state have a different kind of religion in mind, a civic religion called *laïcité*, or secularism.

Secularism goes further than separating church from state or treating religious faith as a private affair. This already is the case, more or less, in Western and indeed non-Western democracies. Secularism is an ideology that must be enforced by a strong state. As the French historian of secularism Jean Baubérot said about his country: "Nation, constitution, law, became 'sacred things.'"[36] Some patriotic French citizens like to claim that *laïcité* is a French exception, a unique product of French Enlightenment philosophes and the French Revolution. In fact, forms of *laïcité* exist in other countries, too, in Turkey and Mexico, for example.

But it is certainly true that France has been a great promoter and exporter of secularism. In France itself, it has been hotly contested since the revolution. One could say that the imposition of secularism caused a kind of civil war to simmer at least until the end of World War II. The relations between the Catholic Church and the French state went through many stages in the last century, ranging from violence to accommodation to formal separation. Some Catholic conservatives continued to see the revolution as a punishment from God. And yet, for many years after the revolution, the church was still seen as the main normative institution for moral behavior. This enraged the radical proponents of *laïcité*, of course, who were ever ready to see the black robes of priests flapping behind everything they regarded as backward and obscurantist (an attitude shared, for obvious reasons, by many liberals and leftists in Italy and Spain).

And not for nothing. The restoration of Catholic authority was always one of the aims of French enemies of the republican state. One of the first acts of Marshall Pétain when he became head of the pro-German Vichy state in 1940 was to challenge *laïcité*, which he called decadent, by ordering public schools to teach "Duties towards God." The active persecution of Jews and Freemasons was, among many other things, also an abandonment of *laïcité*. In 1946, a year after Pétain was sentenced to death (commuted to life by General de Gaulle), *laïcité* was written in the French constitution: "France is a republic, indivisible, secular, democratic, and social."

It is against this background of more than a hundred years of territorial strife between secular and religious authority that the "affair of the veils" in France should be seen. The veil has a long history, which did not begin with Islam. Persian women of a high class wore them long before the Prophet was born. Even in recent times, the image of the veil, and of women wearing them, has not been stable. When France ruled Muslim countries in North Africa, the veil was seen by Frenchmen as a typical example of oppression, which French civilization (*laïcité*) would rectify.[37] Then, in the 1950s, Algerian women wore the veil as a token of resistance against French colonialism and a badge of cultural identity. Frantz Fanon, a fierce opponent of colonialism, wrote in 1958: "In the beginning the veil was a mechanism of resistance, but its value for the social group remained very strong. The veil was worn because tradition demanded a rigid separation of the sexes but also because the occupier was bent on unveiling Algeria."[38]

This is not how many French people saw things in October 1989, the bicentennial year of the French Revolution, when three Muslim girls were expelled from their school in Creil, about thirty miles outside Paris, for refusing to take off their veils. Scarves would be a better word. They did not cover their faces, just part of their heads. As in the Netherlands, when similar controversies break out, images of World War II are immediately invoked. Five well-known philosophers warned about "the Munich of the republican school." This was countered by other, equally heated, phrases, such as "the Vichy of integration."

The "affair" cooled down somewhat when the Council of State, the highest administrative court in France, ruled that wearing signs of religious affiliation was permissible as long as it was discreet and not imposed on others. The affair flared up again in 1994 when the same former principal of the school in Creil, Eugène Chénière, demanded a complete ban on "ostentatious" signs of religious affiliation. François Bayrou, the education minister, decreed that the ban would be imposed. After "Munich" and "Vichy" it was now the turn of the Dreyfus Affair to be recalled. A minority was being persecuted, said the modern Dreyfusards. There should be no tolerance of intolerance, said their opponents. The existence of the republic was deemed to be at stake. The Council of State upheld its earlier decision that discretion should be used and each case judged on its merit.

But the affair refused to die. In 2004, two girls of Jewish origin who had converted to Islam would not take off their scarves or even replace them with less "ostentatious" headwear. Again opponents and proponents accused one another of racism, oppressing women's rights, bringing back Nazism, or Maoism, or totalitarianism. In the end, the so-called Stasi Commission issued a report that advised a ban on all ostentatious religious garb in public schools. The law is often called "the headscarf law" but in fact covers such things as the Jewish kippah and the Sikh turban as well.

What is astonishing is not the debate itself. There are many angles to the headscarf issue: if banning a young woman's right to wear one is wrong, then so is the condoning of men who force their wives and daughters to do so. Strict neutrality—in theory, at least, the foundation of the secular state—is difficult to maintain in times when religious faith is used to justify serious violence. The disquieting thing about the affair is the tone of hysteria, as though a headscarf, worn by members of a religious minority, represented a similar threat to the secular republic as the full might of the eighteenth-century Catholic Church. This hysteria points to deeper anxieties, which the "natives" have in common with immigrants, or their offspring, anxieties about identity in the modern world.

The challenge posed by Muslims in Europe, then, is not cultural, civilizational, or even, in the end, religious. It is social and political. The challenge is how to accommodate communities, whether they be Muslims, Christians, Jews, Sikhs, or any other group of believers, who wish to assert their own norms and beliefs in public. Forcing people to conform to norms set by the state, as is the tendency in France, is illiberal, to say the least. Encouraging people to stick to their own ways, as has been the tendency in Britain, does not foster a sense of inclusion. The way forward, then, is not to insist on social, let alone theological, conformity, but on observance of the law and of the basic rules of democratic society. As long as people play by the rules of free speech, free expression, independent judiciaries, and free elections, they are democratic citizens, whatever they choose to wear on their heads.

•   •   •

If citizens are to play by the rules of democracy, there has to be a common view that those rules are not only just but worth defending. Not all Muslims share this view. Some fundamentalists refuse to recognize the legitimacy of the secular state. This is true of some ultra-orthodox Jews as well, hence their exemption from military service in Israel. There are also Christians who have opted out of mainstream society, especially, but not exclusively, in the United States. Religious communities of this kind live in enclaves, such as Meir Sharim in Jerusalem, or parts of Brooklyn, or rural Pennsylvania. They often consider themselves to be a chosen people who believe, as the Amish do, that, since the world is filled with sinners, "friendship with the world is enmity with God" (James 4:4). But they do not necessarily wish to destroy that world or impose their own beliefs and ways of life on others. In this limited sense, they still play by the rules.

Revolutionaries who dream of wrecking societies they regard as wicked are in a different category. Religious fundamentalism does not have to lead to this type of revolutionary violence. Orthodoxy of faith and political extremism can be linked, but they are not the same thing. There is little point in trying to argue with the revolutionaries. The use of violence in a democracy, for whatever reason, can only be met with force. Popper was right about that. But containment of revolutionary violence will only be successful if the revolutionaries are isolated and deprived of sympathy from the nonviolent believers. The borders between the faithful, including the fundamentalists, and those who will kill for their faith have to be firmed up.

A common solution, favored by many well-meaning liberals, is to find the religious "moderates" and deal with them as if they were leaders of a kind, in effect by putting them in a privileged position. Dealing with one organization, as the central representative of a particular religious community, is a French republican tradition. This might just have worked for the Jewish community. It won't really do for the Muslims, who are much too diverse to be gathered happily under one roof. Milli Görüs, Turkish in origin, is very different from the Algerian Islamic Salvation Front (FIS), which is also quite different from, and indeed hostile to, the equally Algerian Mosque of Paris. Aside from the internal differences, any organization that deals directly with the state risks losing street credibility among the believers, who sense, sometimes with good reason, political opportunism in such contacts. This is equally true in countries with a more laissez-faire approach to religious organization, such as Britain and the Netherlands. Even individual Muslims, who stand for political office or rise in the ranks of the civil service, are quickly accused of "selling out" to promote their own interests.

Trying to find religious "moderates" may not be a good idea anyway. A democratic state has no business being an arbiter in theological affairs. Otherwise, what is the point of separating church from state? All major religions are fundamentalist in the sense of claiming absolute truth. When the current pope was still Cardinal Ratzinger, head of the Congregation for the Doctrine of the Faith, he was adamant that there was only one truth, and that was God's truth.[39] The Catholic Church, not to mention millions of evangelical Protestants in the United States, are against making abortion legal. But most—alas, not all—anti-abortionists still agree to abide by the laws. It is fruitless to enter into theological disputes. Leave that to the religious. *Laïcité*, as Olivier Roy observes, "does not have to do with the acceptance of shared values, but ... with the acceptance of the shared rules of the game."[40]

One of the most controversial and hated figures to have emerged from the Muslim debates in Europe is Tariq Ramadan, a Swiss-born intellectual and activist whose presence has been as polarizing as Ayaan Hirsi Ali's. Those who regard any degree of skepticism toward the latter as a betrayal of Enlightenment values tend to see any sympathy for the former as a sign of the same thing. In fact, it should be possible to see merit in both Hirsi Ali's critique of religious bigotry and Tariq Ramadan's attempt to reconcile Islam with democratic practices. What makes Ramadan such a tricky figure is the apparent discrepancy between his religious orthodoxy and his neo-Marxist politics.

He calls himself a *salafi* reformist. A *salafi* insists on referring to the original holy texts, unencrusted by later commentaries, as an ethical basis for all his actions, whether they be religious, social, or political. Ramadan, in this sense, is a *salafi*, but he advocates the use of reason in the interpretation of these texts to make them relevant to contemporary life. The aim, he writes, "is to protect the Muslim identity and religious practice, to recognize the Western constitutional structure, to become involved as a citizen at the social level, and to live with true loyalty to the country to which one belongs."[41]

A handsome, charismatic, highly media-friendly figure with personal access to many European politicians, Ramadan has contempt for organizations that promote special interests and minority rights for the Muslims. Islam, in his view, should not be just a personal expression of faith, merely adding one more color to the patchwork of cultural and social pluralism. Nor, of course, should it signify an ethnic minority. Muslims, in the West, should not be treated, or ask to be treated, as a minority at all. Ramadan believes that the universalistic values of Islam, as revealed in the holy texts, should not be relativized but put to full use in Western democracies. Indeed, Islam has a special role to play in restoring spirituality to the rationalistic, materialistic world order, which, in his words, "seems to have forgotten the Creator and to depend on a logic that is almost exclusively economic."[42]

This is not an unusual position for a religious person to take. Pope Benedict XVI shares Ramadan's belief that the modern world has made false idols of money and possessions. But Ramadan's fierce criticism of the modern world order, unlike the pope's, is fueled by rhetoric of the Left: on Third World liberation, on U.S. imperialism, the World Bank and IMF, Zionism, and so on. This has given him a following among the remnants of the New Left in France and among people who may not share his belief in Allah but approve of his politics toward Israel and the United States. One of the factors that gravely weakened the Left in recent decades, apart from the sudden collapse of the Soviet Empire, is the abdication of universalism and internationalism in favor of identity politics, focusing on race, gender, and sexual practices. Ramadan seeks to give leftist causes a universal appeal once again through what he sees as the universalism of his Muslim faith.

Linking Islam to Marxism is not a new idea. The twentieth-century Iranian thinker Ali Shari'ati saw religion (Shiite Islam in his case) as a way to liberate the Third World masses from Western imperialism and "market fetishism." Although not an orthodox Marxist, he used Marxist ideology to analyze the ills of modern society and saw Islam as the cure.

Following a similar path, Tariq Ramadan enraged his opponents and delighted many of his supporters by turning the tables on his most prominent critics. In 2003, he launched a well-publicized attack on "French Jewish intellectuals," including Bernard-Henri Lévy, Bernard Kouchner, and Pierre-André Taguieff (who is not in fact Jewish), accusing them of "relativizing the defence of universal principles of equality and justice"[43] by becoming defenders of Israeli interests at the expense of the suffering Palestinians. In other words, the "Jewish" liberals had become sectarians, while Ramadan's Islamism was the new model of universal Enlightenment values.

Exactly why it is a sign of universalism for a European Muslim activist to defend the interests of Palestinians, while it is sectarian for European Jews to defend the interests of Israel, was never made quite clear. And some of the methods used by Ramadan to attack Zionism are dubious. When the Turin Book Fair wished to honor the sixtieth anniversary of the state of Israel in 2008 by inviting Israeli authors such as Amos Oz and David Grossman, Ramadan called for a boycott. In typical fashion, he stated that this was not an Arab or Islamic matter but a universal issue of human rights. Zionism is not the only target of Ramadan's wrath. In 1994, he protested against the staging in Geneva of Voltaire's play *Fanaticism, or Mahomet the Prophet*. The play was dropped.

Still, however misguided some of his interventions may be, Ramadan has renounced the use of violence. Responding to critics who see him as a dangerous figure, he says: "The danger of my discourse in France is that I'm telling people to be citizens. Muslims are still treated as aliens. I'm telling them to vote."[44] So why do so many people (not just "Jewish intellectuals") see him as a menace? It is partly a matter of family connections. Ramadan's standing in the world of Sunni Islam is heightened by the fact that his maternal grandfather was Hassan al-Banna, founder in 1928 of the Muslim Brotherhood in Egypt. Tariq's father, Said Ramadan, was al-Banna's disciple, who, after fleeing

Egypt, became the Brotherhood's representative in Europe. Tariq's brother, Hani Ramadan, who runs the Islamic Center in Geneva, is a controversial preacher who publicly defended the practice of stoning adulterous women.

Tariq Ramadan is highly respectful of his family, especially his revered grandfather. But this does not mean that he wants to establish—as the Muslim Brothers do—a Muslim state. Indeed, he claims that "there is no such thing as an Islamic order. We have to act to promote justice and inject our ethics into the existing system."[45] But since he aims to influence Muslims, especially educated European Muslims, Ramadan is often accused of saying different things to different audiences. This would fit nicely with the rather Trotskyist methods of many Muslim Brothers, who hope to achieve their goals through participation and infiltration rather than direct confrontation. And yet the accusation may be missing the point.

In 2003, Ramadan was confronted on French television by Nicolas Sarkozy, who was then interior minister. Sarkozy challenged Ramadan to come clean on the question of stoning as a punishment for adultery. Stoning is stipulated in the section of the Islamic penal code known as *huddud*. Did or did not Ramadan think this law should be scrapped? Instead of answering with a straight affirmative, Ramadan outraged Sarkozy, and doubtless many television viewers, by calling for a moratorium instead of a ban. "Personally," he said, "I'm against capital punishment, not only in Muslim countries, but also in the U.S. But when you want to be heard in Muslim countries, when you are addressing religious issues, you can't just say it has to stop. *I* think it has to stop. But you have to discuss it within the religious context. There are texts involved. I am not just talking to Muslims in Europe, but addressing the implementation of *huddud* everywhere, in Indonesia, Pakistan and the Middle East. And I'm speaking from the inside to Muslims. Speaking as an outsider would be counterproductive."[46]

This can read in different ways. One might interpret it as a candid affirmation of what Ramadan's critics have thought all along: that he tailors his message to suit his audience. But to expect such candor from such a shrewd activist might be a trifle too naïve. Olivier Roy sees Ramadan's position on corporal punishment as a de facto acceptance of secularism. What he means is that Ramadan, by wishing to leave a religious law for discussion without actually applying it, is disassociating religious doctrine from political or social practice. As Roy puts it: "An approach of this kind maintains orthodoxy while enabling the believer to live in a society governed by *laïcité*."[47] In other words, it allows an orthodox Muslim to play by the rules of democracy without relinquishing his faith.

Perhaps this is conceding a little too much to the demands of religious orthodoxy. If Ramadan is speaking as a European Muslim, then why compromise on a principle in order to "address" the Middle East? And the number of European Muslims in favor of stoning people to death is probably limited. But Ramadan's position, however ambiguous, does not make him a terrorist. And he certainly does not argue anywhere for the implementation of the *huddud*. On the contrary. In this sense, Ramadan draws a clear distinction between his own politics and religious orthodoxy.

The Islamists have merged their politics with their faith. There is no reason to follow their example. Religion and politics should be prised apart. If political violence is simply blamed on the "backwardness" of Islam or the intolerance of the devout, it will become difficult to isolate the revolutionaries from the believers, including fundamentalists, who are prepared to observe the laws of secular society. Violent Islamism is a political problem that cannot be solved with the rhetoric or attitudes of *Kulturkampf*.

Kulturkampf tends to produce the opposite results from those intended. When Bismarck launched his culture war against the Catholics in the 1870s, it strengthened the sense of community among the Catholic believers and made many Protestants feel sullied. In the words of one Protestant theologian: "The state cannot conduct a war against a large part of its own population without causing, on all sides, profound injury to the moral consciousness."[48] Bismarck, in his wisdom, abandoned the war inside his German Reich. But in the Polish lands, then controlled by Prussia, which Bismarck and subsequent German leaders hoped to "Germanize" by encouraging German settlements, the cultural battles continued until, under Nazi occupation, they exploded in a campaign of mass murder.

History never repeats itself precisely. The nations of contemporary Europe are not the same as nineteenth-century Germany, nor are the modern European Muslims much like the Catholics of Bismarck's time. But human impulses toward violence, bigotry, and religious worship are more constant. Muslims in the West must be treated as fellow citizens, just as Catholics were in Protestant Europe. Europeans found a way to reconcile Catholics, Protestant, Jews, and non-believers by democratic means, but only after centuries of murder and oppression. It is in the interest of everyone, except the violent revolutionaries, that Europe escapes from another round of religious violence. Tocqueville's idea that Islam and democracy cannot survive together must be disproven. This will be a test for Islam, but also for all the rest of us who will have to accept the believers as equals, even when we cannot share their faith.

If Islam is to be accepted as one of Europe's religions, which by sheer force of numbers it already is, then space must be found for its practices, as long as they are lawful. Strict secularists will argue that this space must be kept entirely private; the moment you allow religion to trespass on public territory (schools, swimming pools, and so forth), damage is done to the secular state and thus to the democratic order. In fact, the borderlines between public and private are not as clearly drawn in many countries as they are in the French republic, and even there the shadows of the Catholic Church are still long, even in some public schools. Religious practices and education in Germany and the Netherlands are partly financed from the public purse. This may seem unfair, even noxious, to the unbelievers, but it actually gives the secular state a degree of control.

Does acceptance also imply respect? Why should an atheist respect beliefs that he holds to be absurd, at best? But respect is not the same thing as admiration. One need not feel any respect for religious beliefs, only for the dignity of the believers. This is easy to say, of course, but who decides when that dignity is offended? Mullahs, priests, and self-appointed "community leaders" often have a vested interest in being the arbiters of public discourse. They decide which words are offensive to "their people" and how their beliefs are to be discussed. Tariq Ramadan, for one, is most vulnerable to criticism when he adopts this role.

Liberal democracies are not well served by laws that limit free speech, such as laws against blasphemy or denying the Holocaust or the Armenian genocide (both banned in France). In fact, blasphemy is not included in certain restrictions on the freedom of expression laid down in the European Convention of Human Rights. They only apply to intentional and gratuitous insults or hate speech that is designed to incite violence and discrimination against adherents of a particular religion.

There are ways, however, to respect the dignity of fellow citizens without recourse to the law. In practice, people in civilized societies tend to refrain from using words or expressing opinions that are bound to cause offense. And offense depends to a large extent on who says what to whom and under what circumstances. Criticizing religious beliefs should certainly not be banned by law. Criticism among the believers is in fact a good thing, and such critics must be protected by the law against violent repercussions.

Salman Rushdie made the distinction between attacking beliefs, and attacking believers. The former should be entirely permissible, while the latter is not. This distinction might be lost on some of the believers, who would take an attack on their faith personally. But this is no reason to dismiss Rushdie's claim. It could be sharpened, perhaps, by stressing the legitimacy of attacking religious authorities, especially when their statements have political consequences. When the pope tells people in Africa that condoms encourage AIDS, he should be challenged. The same is obviously true when Muslim clerics make statements that encourage violent acts against women, homosexuals, infidels, or whomever.

Yet it is possible to qualify Rushdie's dictum in one respect, not legally but socially, even politically. Criticism is most useful when it concerns matters that can be rationally debated. Quite apart from the possible offense it might cause, there is not much point in using rational arguments against the belief in God, for it is a belief, not an opinion. Revealed truth can influence the views of an individual, for better or worse, but should not be granted any political authority. Expression of religious beliefs in politics are legitimate as long as those beliefs inform positions that are subject to reason. Martin Luther King's politics, and the way he expressed his views, were deeply affected by his religious beliefs, but his goals were rational. He had turned his religious faith to secular ends. That is why he spoke to non-believers as powerfully as he did to his fellow Christians.

So if one truly believes in the separation of church and state, which all democrats should, a certain discretion about the religious beliefs of others is in order. This need not, and should not, mean virtual segregation, as in the "pillars" that divided Catholics from Protestants in the Netherlands, or in the ideology of multiculturalism. It means what Olivier Roy meant when he spoke about leaving theology to the believers and concentrating on the rules of the democratic game. Confucius, that wise old Chinese sage, had never heard of democracy, but he said more or less the same thing when asked by his disciple how to serve the spirits and gods: Let us leave the spirits aside, until we know how best to serve men.

NOTES

ONE: *Full Tents and Empty Cathedrals*

1. Sinclair Lewis, *Elmer Gantry* (New York: Harcourt, Brace and Company, 1927), 48.
2. Ibid., 432.
3. Zev Chafets, "Late-Period Limbaugh," *New York Times Magazine*, July 6, 2008.
4. Alexis de Tocqueville, *Democracy in America*, trans. Arthur Goldhammer (New York: Library of America, 2004), 293.
5. Ibid., 295.
6. Ibid., 449.
7. Ibid, 295.
8. Ibid., 298.
9. Ibid., 301.
10. Thomas Jefferson, *Notes on the State of Virginia* (1781), Query XVII.
11. Frank Lambert, *Religion in American Politics* (Princeton: Princeton University Press, 2008), 22.
12. Tocqueville, *Democracy in America*, 288.
13. David Hume, "Essay X: Of Superstition and Enthusiasm," in *Essays Moral, Political, and Literary*, ed. Eugene F. Miller (1742–54; Indianapolis: Liberty Fund, 1987).
14. Thomas Hobbes, *Leviathan*, XIII.9.
15. Mark Lilla, *The Stillborn God: Religion, Politics, and the Modern West* (New York: Knopf, 2007).
16. Spinoza, *Tractatus Theologico-Politicus*, 15.
17. Ibid., chapter XI.1.
18. Ibid., chapter III.10.
19. Jonathan I. Israel, *Enlightenment Contested: Philosophy, Modernity, and the Emancipation of Man, 1670–1752* (New York: Oxford University Press, 2006).

20. Ibid., 247.

21. Secularism is not the same as secular; one denotes an ideology, the other describes a state of being.

22. *The Social Contract*, book 1. See *The Living Thoughts of Rousseau*, presented by Romain Rolland (Philadelphia: D. McKay, 1939).

23. Quoted by Conor Cruise O'Brien in "The Decline and Fall of the French Revolution," *New York Review of Books*, February 15, 1990.

24. Ibid.

25. Quoted by Isaiah Berlin in "Joseph de Maistre and the Origins of Fascism: II," *New York Review of Books*, October 11, 1990.

26. Isaiah Berlin, "Joseph de Maistre and the Origins of Fascism," *New York Review of Books*, September 27, 1990.

27. Tocqueville, *Democracy in America*, 289.

28. Quoted in Richard Hofstadter, *The American Political Tradition and the Men Who Made It* (New York: Vintage Books, 1989), 38.

29. See Lambert, *Religion in American* Politics, 36.

30. Jeroen Koch, *Abraham Kuyper* (Amsterdam: Boom, 2007), 201.

31. Lambert, *Religion in American Politics*, 170.

T W O : Oriental Wisdom

1. Israel, *Enlightenment Contested*, 641.

2. Ibid.

3. Voltaire, *Works*, vol. 15, part 2, p. 180, quoted in Jyoti Mohan, "La civilisation la plus antique: Voltaire's Images of India," *Journal of World History* 16, no. 2 (2005): 173–85.

4. Voltaire, *The Philosophical Dictionary*, selected and translated by H. I. Woolf (New York: Knopf, 1924).

5. Voltaire, *The Philosophical Dictionary*, trans. and ed. Peter Gay, vol. 1 (New York: Basic Books, 1962).

6. Quoted in Mohan, "Voltaire's Images of India," 179.

7. Voltaire, *Philosophical Dictionary*, trans. Gay, vol. 1.

8. *The Analects of Confucius*, trans. Simon Leys (New York: Norton, 1997), 50.

9. Ibid., 6.

10. Tocqueville, *Democracy in America*, 308.

11. *The Analects of Confucius*, xxv.

12. Voltaire, *Philosophical Dictionary*, trans. Gay, vol. 1.

13. Much of this information comes from Jonathan Spence, *The Search for Modern China*, 2nd ed. (New York: Norton, 1999). Spence also wrote a brilliant biography of Hong, *God's Chinese Son: The Taiping Heavenly Kingdom of Hong Xiuquan* (New York: Norton, 1996).

14. Quoted in Kenneth Lieberthal, *Governing China: From Revolution through Reform* (New York: Norton, 2003), 195.

15. Spence, *The Search for Modern China*, 232.

16. *Min Pao*, December 2, 1906, reprinted in *Prescriptions for Saving China: Selected Writings of Sun Yat-sen*, ed. Julie Lee Wei, Ramon H. Myers, and Donald G. Gillin (Stanford: Hoover Institution Press, 1994), 41.

17. Ibid., 88.

18. Spence, *The Search for Modern China*, 303.

19. See Bob Tadashi Wakabayashi, *Anti-Foreignism and Western Learning in Early-Modern Japan* (Cambridge, MA: Council of East Asian Studies, Harvard University, 1986).

20. Ibid., 123.

21. Ibid., 143.

22. Quoted in Carol Gluck, *Japan's Modern Myths* (Princeton: Princeton University Press, 1985), 133.

23. Ian Buruma, *Inventing Japan* (New York: Random House, 2003), 38.

24. See John Dower, *Embracing Defeat* (New York: Norton, 1999).

THREE: Enlightenment Values

1. Tocqueville, *Democracy in America*, 445.

2. See Israel, *Enlightenment Contested*.

3. Olivier Roy, *Secularism Confronts Islam* (New York: Columbia University Press, 2007), xi.

4. Quoted in Shiv Malik, "My Brother the Bomber," *Prospect* 135 (June 2007).

5. Ibid.

6. Melanie Phillips, *Londonistan* (London: Encounter Books, 2006), 64.

7. Ibid., 66.

8. Melanie Phillips is by no means alone in her defection from the Left. Such Parisian veterans of the 1968 student rebellion as Pascal Bruckner, André Glucksmann, and Bernard-Henri Lévy have followed a similar path.

9. Phillips, *Londonistan*, 62.

10. Bruce Bawer, *While Europe Slept: How Radical Islam Is Destroying the West from Within* (New York: Doubleday, 2006).

11. Tom Gross in the *New York Post*, June 18, 2006.

12. Roy, *Secularism Confronts Islam*, 31.

13. Phillips, *Londonistan*, 70.

14. *Volkskrant*, February 9, 2002.

15. Phillips, *Londonistan*, 11.

16. These events are well described in Gilles Kepel, *Allah in the West: Islamic Movements in America and Europe* (Stanford: Stanford University Press, 1997).

17. See http://www.KenanMalik.com. A version of this article appeared in Kenan Malik, "Born in Bradford," *Prospect* 115 (October 2005).

18. Norman Podhoretz, "My Negro Problem—and Ours," *Commentary* (February 1963): 93–101.

19. Ibid., 99.

20. David Edgar, *The Guardian*, April 19, 2008.

21. Ibid.

22. Ayaan Hirsi Ali, *Infidel* (New York: Free Press, 2007), 296.

23. Ibid., 272.

24. Petition to support Ayaan Hirsi Ali, 2006, http://www.petitiononline.com/AyaanHir/.

25. Reported on Dutch World Service, Radio Nederland Omroep, February 11, 2008.

26. Sam Harris and Salman Rushdie, "Ayaan Hirsi Ali: Abandoned to Fanatics," *Los Angeles Times*, October 9, 2007.

27. *Volkskrant*, January 28, 2008.

28. Geert Wilders, *Elsevier Magazine*, December 27, 2007.

29. In fact, as Benjamin Kaplan argues in *Divided by Faith: Religious Conflict and the Practice of Toleration in Early Modern Europe* (Cambridge, MA: Harvard University Press, 2007), tolerance of other religions was already widely practiced before the Enlightenment.

30. John Locke, *A Letter Concerning Toleration* (1689), translated from Latin by William Popple (New York: Routledge, 1991).

31. Pascal Bruckner, "On Identity," *Onwards and Forwards*, January 27, 2007, http://onwardsandforwards.wordpress.com/2007/01/.

32. Ian Buruma, *Murder in Amsterdam: The Death of Theo van Gogh and the Limits of Tolerance* (New York: Penguin, 2006).

33. Leon de Winter, review of *Murder in Amsterdam: The Death of Theo van Gogh and the Limits of Tolerance* by Ian Buruma, *Wall Street Journal*, September 9, 2006.

34. Karl Popper, *The Open Society and Its Enemies* (Princeton: Princeton University Press, 1971), 265.

35. Phillips, *Londonistan*, 189.

36. Jean Baubérot, *Histoire de la laïcité en France* (Paris: Presses Universitaires de France, 2000).

37. See Joan Wallach Scott, *The Politics of the Veil* (Princeton: Princeton University Press, 2007).

38. Quoted in ibid., 64.

39. Roy, *Secularism Confronts Islam*, 38.

40. Ibid.

41. Tariq Ramadan, *Western Muslims and the Future of Islam* (New York: Oxford University Press, 2003), 27.

42. Ibid., 73.

43. First published online on http://www.oumma.com/ in October 2003, and later in the Geneva newspaper *Le Courrier*, October 8, 2003.

44. Ian Buruma, "Tariq Ramadan Has an Identity Issue," *New York Times Magazine*, February 4, 2007.

45. Ibid.

46. Ibid.

47. Roy, *Secularism Confronts Islam*, 45.

48. Gordon A. Craig, *The Germans* (New York: Penguin, 1984), 94.